The Heart
of the Matter

Reflections of a Very Sick Man

Bruce Talbot

Editing and design by RavenMark
Back cover photo by Bill Brawley

All proceeds from *The Heart of Matter* are donated to the Bruce Talbot Fund for Parkinson's patients in Vermont. For more information about the Bruce Talbot Fund, please contact Judith Talbot Sutphen at jtsutphen@gmail.com.

For copies or permissions, please contact:

Judith Talbot Sutphen

jsutphen@gmail.com

ISBN 978-0-9713998-3-9

This book is for my family, dedicated with great love . . .

To my older son, Peter . . . who said, as a cool 16-year-old riding in the car with me, his decidedly uncool father, to New York for the 2000 Parkinson's Unity Walk, "Dad, there isn't anything I wouldn't do for you." He meant it.

To my younger son, Alex . . . who, at age 8 went door to door throughout our little village and collected more than $1,400 for Parkinson's research. (No neighbor was safe!)

To my daughter, Fia . . . "La Contenta" ("the Happy One" they called her in her native country of Guatemala), who always makes me smile and laugh, a huge gift for which I'm exceedingly grateful.

And to my wife, Judith . . . a truly extraordinary human being who has walked with me every CLUMP/slide, CLUMP/slide step of my Parkinson's trek; who has never hesitated to kick me in the keister when it looked like I was gearing up for a good mope; who has never lowered the great expectations she holds for me; who has somehow managed to continue leading a demanding and remarkable life; and who, most incredibly, makes no bones about the fact that she loves me ridiculously. I return that ridiculous love many times over.

Contents

Foreword

A little over 16 years ago in the fall of 1994, Bruce Talbot developed a tremor in his left thumb—an early sign of the development of Parkinson's disease. In 1817, James Parkinson himself recognized the insinuating nature of the disease when he wrote ". . . so imperceptible are the inroads of this malady." In Bruce's essay "Embracing Our Inner Alien," which became the first chapter of this book, he employs his wonderful journalistic talent and sense of humor and puts his own twist on recognizing the early symptoms:

> When we reach our 40s, body parts start to twitch. We run too far, our legs twitch. We read too late, our eyelids twitch. So, it was with no particular alarm and even some amusement that in the late fall of 1994 I noticed the webbing between the thumb and forefinger of my left hand twitching dramatically, like Sigourney Weaver's Alien-inhabited torso in the thriller film of the same name.

The essay goes on to tell about how Bruce came to grips with the alien thing that was taking over his body and how he "edged in sideways to a diagnosis."

I met Bruce and Judith after they had investigated every angle of medicine—Eastern and Western—and I was the one who gave him the "unequivocal verdict" that he had Parkinson's disease. But rather than curling up and letting the disease take over his life, Bruce responded in a remarkable way. The so-called verdict, he wrote, "gave me my bearings as I began navigating through life with a major chronic illness. I had presented myself for diagnosis knowing that even if the news were to be the worst possible, I could, in some way, get a hold on my illness. I could somehow begin dealing with it, loosening its grip on me."

In the essays throughout *The Heart of the Matter*, Bruce reflects on how one can gain insights from illness and disease that can transform a struggle into a discovery of what is important. In this deeply personal journey, Bruce actually provides the outline of how to deal with life in general . . . the explicit and implicit analogies, metaphors, and allegories. Take his metaphor of a tuna fish sandwich as a way to talk about fulfillment, or the mule in the well story that illustrates perseverance, or the proverbial Vermont mud season as a way of looking at getting out of the ruts we find ourselves in—sick or well. The joys, the challenges, and the quagmires of life are all lessons, in a way, in "The Tao of Talbot."

I have always felt privileged and honored as a physician and neurologist to be in a field of service to patients and families challenged by diseases of the nervous system. Neurological diseases are not easy—to say the least. The incredible strengths and core values that come to the surface when we are challenged are readily apparent in the patients and families who are faced with the challenges of Parkinson's disease. Bruce Talbot was emblematic; he was the poster child—if you will—for Parkinson's disease. He exemplified the wonderful can-do attitude that is critical to help the field move forward. He took the bit between his teeth and never stopped moving forward in his efforts to advance the cause of a cure for Parkinson's disease and improve the lives of patients. Even when Bruce was in the throes of dying from brain cancer, his indomitable spirit, humor, and love of life were ever present.

Bruce's last gift to the world is this book. It is for people who are ill, yes, but it is also for people who are well and want to live better. There are many lessons within this book, but two themes are constant: (1) Identify and value the positives in life; and (2) Do not miss out on love. Bruce loved life and loved people. He made this very plain to me when he said one time, "I love you, and there is nothing you can do about it." These are words physicians generally do not hear from their patients. I always felt, and eventually told Bruce, that there was absolutely nothing I wanted to do about his loving me.

> – *Dr. Robert Hamill*
> *Chair of Neurology, University of Vermont Medical School*

Preface

On a raw, rainy Saturday afternoon in the late 1980s, I was poking around an old downtown section of Baltimore, wary of a city that I had been told had a rough edge. I was in town to attend (as humor columnist Dave Barry would put it, I'm not making this up) *a tombstone industry convention*. During the first day's late afternoon session, I slipped out of the conference center and headed downtown. At the time, I was manager of public relations for the trade association representing the granite quarrying, sawing, and finishing companies of the Barre, Vermont, stone industry, which had as its primary product line cemetery memorials. (Our unofficial industry slogan was, "We'll be the last to let you down.") The Barre stone industry was floundering, and so was I. The stone industry was looking for new markets, and I was yearning for work that would light me up. Tombstones weren't doing it for me. That dismal afternoon in Baltimore—about five years before the onset of my first Parkinson's symptoms—I was alone and lonely and wondering what I was doing with my life and, more immediately and practically, what other job I could do back in Vermont, my job-poor state, if I decided to bail out.

While exploring Baltimore, still a grand if tattered old East Coast port city, I ducked out of the rain into a bookstore. That day, at the end of the first aisle, one title stood out for me, *The Wisdom of Insecurity*, philosopher Alan Watts' treatise on living contentedly in this age of looming cataclysm. I was on the cusp of age 40 and feeling considerable insecurity but coming up short on *wisdom*. I was divorced, paying (very willingly) a hard-to-shoulder amount of child support, at times feeling isolated, at other times reveling in my seclusion. I also felt stuck because I knew that for my own happiness and well-being I would have to quit what was one of the few halfway decent-paying journalism/PR-centered jobs in Vermont.

That day in Baltimore, I, in my typical fashion, scoured the bookstore, yet I kept returning to the philosophy section to eyeball Watts' book. Watts had snagged me with his book's bewildering title. It kept gnawing at me. *The Wisdom of Insecurity*, eh? The specter of—through the book—coming face to face with my insecurities made me very uneasy; still, I was lured by the possibility that within my insecurity could be something of value. I pulled Watts' slim paperback from the store shelf, paid for it, and put it on my own shelf back home where it sat unread for 15 years. Fearful of discovering some overwhelming, fundamental flaw in the way I was living my life, I didn't dare crack the book all that time, only occasionally taking furtive notice of that strange title. Those glances alone gave me more than my money's worth, over time provoking myriad unsettling thoughts, questions, and realizations. First off, I realized that it is oftentimes in that place where certainty is absent and insecurity rules that the deepest and most vital and sincere questions typically surface.

Like most other people, I've craved security in my life. I've sought respite in head-in-the-sand not-knowing-ness. I've lusted for comfortableness. But I know now that it has been in the uncomfortable place of uncertainty that I've confronted my most important questions and reaped my greatest rewards, where I've gotten powerful new perspectives on my life. Dealing with the unknown has been an unexpected blessing.

By the 1990s, I had received the news that I had Parkinson's disease. My symptoms began on my left side with severe rigidity. Fortunately, I'm right-handed, although for some quirky neurological reason, my handwriting began to shrink dramatically. My neurologist told me that because the human body wants to be symmetrical, my symptoms would be pretty evenly distributed on both sides. I move slowly ("gingerly," as a friend puts it) as I shuffle along. A couple of years ago, my voice took a cue from Muhammad Ali's and softened to a hoarse whisper. (Therapy has helped me learn to project.) I've also developed some tremors in my hands and arms. I feel like I'm shivering without being cold. I fear choking and aspirating food. My throat muscles no longer contract normally, and I have trouble swallowing. Aspirating food and resultant pneumonia is what usually kills the few people who die from Parkinson's disease.

Since the onset of Parkinson's, I've come think that perhaps it is illness that forces us to recognize life's ephemeral nature and release our feelings. I don't know. I do know that my illness comes with a common yet highly embarrassing side effect—and I love it. All it takes to move me and make me choke up is something as simple and sappy as that phone company TV commercial where the son comes home for the holidays on leave from the army. I watch it and in no time I'm a blubbering mess. I've learned subsequently that many people with my disease, like me, have suffered diminished empathy-controlling capacity.

For most of us who are sick, the old order has to crumble around us before we become willing to honestly, heroically examine our lives and feel the world intensely. The world of chronic illness is a place of insecurity.

"What's happening to me?" we may have thought or asked (or screamed) at the onset of new, odd, perhaps frightening, perhaps unbearable symptoms. "What's going to happen to me?"

Only two years ago did I finally say, "What the hell!" and read *The Wisdom of Insecurity* and encounter Watts' revolutionary conclusion: that the highest happiness, greatest insight, and most solid certitude are found only in our awareness that impermanence and insecurity are inescapable and inseparable from life.

I hope the thoughts and experiences written here are nourishing to those who are sick and thought provoking to those who are well.

– Bruce Talbot
January 2010

Embracing Our Inner Alien

When we reach our 40s, body parts start to twitch. We run too far, our legs twitch. We read too late, our eyelids twitch. So, it was with no particular alarm and even some amusement that in the late fall of 1994 I noticed the webbing between the thumb and forefinger of my left hand twitching dramatically, like Sigourney Weaver's Alien-inhabited torso in the thriller film of the same name.

Over the ensuing months, my hand became increasingly stiff and I became increasingly alarmed. Much of what I was doing for work at the time—public relations—required me to use a computer . . . that is, to type. When I would force my left hand to stretch toward far-flung keys like A and B and Z, I would get woozy and nauseated. The work for which I was trained was literally making me sick.

❋

I edged in sideways to a diagnosis.

My first stop—hoping for a comfortable-to-bear explanation—was a naturopath. No answers. I saw a chiropractor, hoping the solution might be the realignment of a few vertebrae. It wasn't.

Reluctantly, facing up to the possibility that something truly significant was going on, I took the obvious but dreaded next step and saw a neurologist. The doctor took my left hand as if to shake it and, instead, rotated it around the axis of my left wrist. He rotated my entire arm like the drive rods that turn the wheels of a train. The arm jerked like a cogwheel. He had me walk back and forth across his office. Like the Frankenstein monster's CLUMP/slide, CLUMP/slide, my gait was clumsy. Then he gave me the tentative news: "You have possible early onset of Parkinson's disease."

That day, the planet shifted. Nothing in my universe would ever be the same. I learned that slowly yet persistently, my brain was dying.

Sorry to be so melodramatic, but it's true. Now, mind you, the *whole thing* wasn't dying. The section responsible for thinking up reasons for not doing yard work, for example, functioned better than ever. The dying part is a tiny area called the *substantia nigra*, which produces the chemical dopamine that transmits brain signals that control movement. That made me one of the estimated one million Americans and untold millions of others around the world with what is, thanks to the diagnoses of high-profile patients such as actor Michael J. Fox and former world heavyweight champion Muhammad Ali, one of the newer, "in" chronic diseases.

❋

In 1994 when I was diagnosed, however, Parkinson's wasn't "in" at all. Generally, it was thought of as a fairly inconsequential malady that gave the elderly the shakes and resigned them to quietly padding around the house. When Parkinson's knocked at my door, I was 45, and it threatened me with the possibility that, as it progressed, it could incapacitate me with tremors, yank my body with violent jerking, stiffen my face into a mask, and trigger depression and even dementia. At worst, I could become a prisoner in my own body, conscious but unable to move.

Being a reasonably normal individual, my first reaction to my diagnosis was grim. "This is," came my automatic response, "the beginning of my life going down the tubes." It seemed like a point of view that was all too legitimate, but it left me feeling lousy.

❋

As the neurologist who suspected the early onset of Parkinson's wound up that devastating appointment, he handed me samples of the drug Sinemet. Only through autopsy can a physician actually "see" Parkinson's in the brain, he explained. But you can go a long way toward obtaining a definitive diagnosis, he said, by administering Sinemet, an artificial dopamine, and noting its effect. If you feel better, you probably have Parkinson's. After a week on the medication, I felt dizzy, disorientated—and relieved. However, my neurologist wasn't ready to declare good news. Sinemet wasn't always effective with Parkinson's, he said, and, what's more, we could, instead, be dealing with the after-effects of a stroke or an aneurysm.

Nailing the Diagnosis: East and West

In short order, I found myself in the MRI unit across the Connecticut River from my Vermont home, in New Hampshire at the Dartmouth-Hitchcock Medical Center. Garbed in a hospital johnny, I lay on a narrow plank that slowly eased me inside the colossal machine's suffocatingly tight patient compartment for a lengthy round of magnetic picture-taking. I had not had a stroke, my neurologist reported at my follow-up appointment. But, he said, the MRI had turned up evidence of an old, small, left-sided brain hemorrhage. Because of its location, the leak couldn't be considered a factor affecting my left-sided Parkinson's-like symptoms, but it was worthy of great concern. Simply put, the question was, Would the pipe burst again? Back to Dartmouth-Hitchcock for a better look.

During one of the less-fun mornings of my life, technicians poked a hole into the major artery that courses its way through my groin. Then, like threading a drawstring into the waistband of a pair of sweatpants, they inched a tube up into my aorta until it eventually reached the outskirts of my brain cavity. Through the tube, they injected dye that would make any weak blood vessels readily apparent in X-rays. When the pictures came back, there was good news and more bad news. My blood vessels were intact. And Parkinson's seemed all the more likely.

❋

Not having been helped by Sinemet, I began looking for other treatment approaches. Several people told me about an acupuncturist and practitioner of ancient Chinese medicine who lived across the state in the village of North Bennington. I made an appointment, and a few days later, Judith and I drove an hour and a half over the mountain and a couple of miles down an old dirt road. At my destination, I underwent treatment at the in-home office of this healer of some renown, a former abbot of a Vietnamese Buddhist monastery.

At that first appointment, my soft-spoken new health care provider had me stand, then placed his hands in different locations—especially concentrating on my wrists—in order to take body temperature and pulse readings. After about 10 minutes he stopped, and I asked him the Big One: "Do I have Parkinson's disease?"

"I . . . have . . . never . . . heard . . . of . . . that," he said haltingly, explaining in his limited, heavily accented English that several of my vital organs were "hot," that my entire left side was affected (at the time, that was news to me), and if I didn't get treatment, my whole body eventually would become rigid. I made my second of what would turn out to be a year's worth of appointments. The weekly sessions that followed were much the same: the hands-on taking of my wrist temperatures and pulse; the occasional inspection of my tongue; and an inquiry about my lifestyle status, especially whether or not over the past week I had gotten sufficient "sweat exercise." The healer then would retreat to his back room where, for 10 minutes or so, he would snap, pound, and grind what sounded like twigs and old leaves, reappearing with a bag of decimated herbs that he would present to me at the conclusion of the appointment. Each day for the next week, late in the afternoon, I'd put some of the herbs in a pot of water and cook them down to an indescribably bad-tasting, bitter Chinese brew.

My condition didn't seem to be improving; nor did it seem to be worsening . . . a good and unusual state to be in, in the case of Parkinson's.

❋

Toward the end of the summer, our family moved to northern Vermont. That fall, in Burlington, during a coffee break at a University of Vermont Parkinson's symposium, Judith and I staked out the Danish table and cornered the impressive event moderator, Dr. Robert Hamill, chairman of the university's department of neurology. We asked Dr. Hamill if he would take me on as a patient. He said yes, and in an instant I went from Eastern to Western in my treatment approach. In exchange, I got a definitive Parkinson's diagnosis—a far different experience from getting that elusive "possible" diagnosis a year or so earlier.

My new neurologist's unequivocal verdict gave me my bearings as I began navigating through life with a major chronic illness. I had presented myself for diagnosis knowing that even if the news were to be the worst possible, I could, at least in some way, get a hold on my illness. I could somehow begin dealing with it, loosening its grip on me. I also got prescriptions for some heavy-duty medications that soon had me feeling much better. My CLUMP/slide became more subtle, and I found, much to my surprise and delight, that I was able to easily go 10 or 15 minutes at a stretch without noticing and thinking about my Parkinson's disease (blessed psychological breathing room!). I was also spared the needless expenditure of energy—physical, emotional, and financial—that I might otherwise have squandered by going down the wrong treatment road.

By being diagnosed, I became legitimized. I became an honest-to-God patient.

Dazed and Dispassionate

When I received my original, tentative Parkinson's diagnosis, down in southern Vermont, the notion of a life with the disease had left me dazed. I didn't know *what* to think. But, in a short time, my feelings gelled. Call it shock or profound denial, if you will, but I began reacting as if my diagnosis were some kind of important but cold, dry *information*, and I responded to it accordingly . . . dispassionately. ("Here's what's going on and what might happen," went my thinking. "I'll deal with all that when I need to.") It was almost as if the illness were someone else's.

As for Judith, my diagnosis was immediately devastating. For weeks, she was somber, spending unusually long periods alone. When she would emerge from our bedroom, I would know from her red eyes and flushed face that she had been crying. We'd only been married a year—a second marriage for each of us—and something like Parkinson's disease WASN'T SUPPOSED TO HAPPEN! I tried to push onward while Judith continued to grieve well into the fall. Then, one day while working in the kitchen, she stopped what she was doing, looked at me with a wry grin, and matter-of-factly said, "You know, though, I will like having that handicapped license plate."

It took until about a year after my diagnosis for me to take my ultimately unavoidable emotional plunge. At the time, our family was still living in southern Vermont when Judith got an appointment to a major state government job in Montpelier, Vermont's state capital, 120 miles to the north. For several months, Judith worked part time, commuting to Montpelier for weekly three-day stints while I stayed home with the two young kids we had adopted. One day, alone and vulnerable, I hit bottom. The question—the realization, actually— came rumbling in: Why would Judith want to link her future to that of a partner who was likely to be a sorry playmate if not a crushing burden? When she returned home for the weekend, I let everything pour out.

"How dare you think I could be so small!" she exploded. "How DARE you!" She held me. She said she'd stay with me forever. Then she pulled back, looked at me with a glint in her eye, and said, "But the minute you start drooling, I'm out of here."

We laughed together. And I wondered, could I look at my illness another way, a way that could sustain me through whatever lay ahead?

One Summer Afternoon on a Raft

O n a raft in the middle of a northern Vermont pond, I learned —*really*—what a breakthrough is. It came on a hot summer afternoon in the late 1980s while swimming with my son Peter, and it has given me the ability to transform any experience that may come my way.

Ever since Peter was a year old, we had spent many a day in and around water, starting out that first winter at a fitness club pool. The only downside to our winter swimming was that the pool had been designed for lap swimming and racing without a shallow end—it was not intended for playful little kids. Consequently, Peter did a lot of death-grip hanging on to me. A parent and child can get pretty close, pretty quickly under circumstances like that.

When Peter was 3 and his mother, Martha, and I separated, I moved into a small cottage on the edge of mile-long, gorgeous Curtis Pond. At its southern end, the pond has a sandy beach, a shallow wading area, and not too far out, a raft. Peter loved swimming back and forth between the shore and the raft. He'd either swim alone, tightly lashed into a life jacket, or he'd ride on my back. I was always ready to grab him if he got into trouble, but he never did.

❀

When Peter was 7, we were lying on the pond raft when half a dozen brawny, boisterous young men swam out in a pack to the raft. They proceeded to stampede from one end of the raft to the other, slamming down on the edge, springing into the air, and flipping into the water. After a few minutes, Peter asked me if he could ask one of the "big guys" to teach *him* how to flip. I gulped. One of my inexplicable lifelong fears has been that I, in a feeble attempt to do a flip, would come too close to the edge of the raft or dock or pool deck and crack my head. I could also all-too-vividly picture Peter's head cracked open on the edge of that Curtis Pond raft. *Very* uneasily, I got the assurance of one of the young men that he'd carefully spot Peter as he learned to somersault through the air. In minutes Peter was flipping with the best of them.

Then came the question I dreaded: "Why don't you try it, Dad?"

I swaggered a little and haughtily said, "Dad doesn't flip." Peter didn't seem disappointed and went back to hurtling through the air, but for me that moment was like a stab through the heart. Swimming had been the most fun, closest thing we had done together during those early years. I never considered myself an athlete, but swimming was always something I could do well. Now Peter was moving on, and I was staying behind. I was afraid of injury and—worse—afraid of looking foolish.

The Breakthrough

The following summer, Peter and I were again back on the raft, which had become something of a place of sadness for me. Peter buzzed around doing kid things like rocking the raft and making waves. Eventually, I noticed him kneel at the edge of the raft, tuck his chin into his chest and gently roll headfirst into the water. It dawned on me that Peter's somersaulting was the heart and soul of a flip, and I thought, "I'll bet he could teach *me* to flip."

The notion of asking my then-8-year-old child to teach me how to do what I considered to be a life-threatening feat seemed close to absurd, but I decided the time to learn was then or never. So, I asked. Peter was more than a little incredulous . . . and delighted. He didn't hesitate.

"Sure!" he said.

Before I entrusted my well-being to so young a child, I took a moment to explain the terror-abating practice of breaking down a threatening task into small, less confronting steps.

First, Peter had me kneel at the edge of the raft, tuck, and roll in, as he had been doing. Next, he had me squat and roll in . . . then stand, spring into the air and roll in . . . then take a step and roll in . . . and finally, run, spring off the edge, do a somersault in the air, and plunge in headfirst. I couldn't contain myself. When I came to the surface, like an 8-year-old myself, I shouted, "*Peter, I did it! I did a flip! Thank you, Peter! Thank you!*"

So what are breakthroughs, and why are they important for people who are very sick? When I hear the word breakthrough, I envision that circus routine where the clown loses control of the motorcycle he's riding and bursts through a billboard. Before he loses control of the bike, the clown sees his world—the front of the billboard—one way. After bursting through, the world looks altogether different.

A breakthrough, as I see it, is the bursting through of an obstacle or restriction, and it happens suddenly and often dramatically. A breakthrough, as I use the term, is an achievement that isn't going to happen on its own—you have to cause it. A breakthrough requires courage. It takes effort.

❋

In the field of medicine, as we well know, there have been breakthroughs aplenty, from antiseptics, anesthetics, and antibiotics to the discovery of germs and viruses, immunization, X-rays, MRIs, CT scans, PET scans, laser surgery, the discovery of the so-called mind–body connection, organ transplants, severed limb reattachments . . . the list goes on and on. The breakthroughs that I'm talking about occur within us.

I've become quite clear that I'm a stubborn member of a stubborn species. Or maybe, more precisely, I'm a scared member of a fearful species. We humans don't much like change. We don't like to take risks.

We cling desperately to the status quo, whatever the cost may be.

Accordingly, for us to have a breakthrough in our lives, the old, safe, predictable order has to fall apart. No breakdown, no breakthrough. The status quo has to get too painful or too boring before most of us will snap into breakthrough mode. True, we don't have to wait around for breakdowns to occur. We can make our own, but be well aware that only a small handful of people will ever actually cause their own breakdowns.

Another thing I know is that the bigger the breakdown is, the bigger the potential breakthrough can be. Chronic illness, of course, qualifies as one of those breakdowns that hold the potential for plenty of life-altering breakthroughs.

Breakdowns occur only when we've made commitments, consciously or unconsciously, to ourselves and to others. If we have no commitments, no matter what happens, we'll have no breakdowns. If one of my kids got gravely ill, I'd get terribly upset, to say the least. If, on the other hand, I read in the newspaper that a child I didn't know, living in another part of the world, got seriously ill, I might feel empathy but nothing approaching grief. The difference is that I have an enormous commitment to the well-being of my own children, and I'd do anything I could to help them. As for the other sick kids of the world, I contribute to charities and vote for candidates who endorse generous foreign aid, but I don't go abroad and hold those sick kids.

Why NOW Is the Time for a Breakthrough

My first response to my Parkinson's diagnosis was that my life was beginning an irreversible slide down the tubes. Thankfully, at the time of my diagnosis I was aware enough of my thinking process to see that I was doing my same old thing . . . automatically starting down the path of the glum, resigned defeatist. I was able to transcend that initial bleak outlook and ask myself—more or less in these words: What's a better, more supportive way to look at my new illness?

My process was simple. What made it work was my ability to stop the emotional and cerebral craziness whipping around inside of me. In those periods of serenity, I was free from my usual impulse to nudge and hope and beg and barter with and pray to whomever or whatever is really in charge for the answer I thought I wanted, which was, you won't be surprised to learn, where and how I could get cured. Instead, I got an unexpected answer . . . that my Parkinson's could be a huge contribution—somehow—to the lives of many people, including mine.

❋

It's time for a breakthrough because it's *always* time for a breakthrough. The nature of life is change, and by extension, with change come breakdowns and breakthroughs. At this gravely troubled time in history, we face the prospect of huge breakdowns . . . and the possibility of huge breakthroughs. Do we have the courage to take advantage of these breakdowns? Do we have the courage to realize a breakthrough and possibly our dreams? To flip off a raft?

The Lies We Tell Ourselves

I make up a lot of stuff.

I exaggerate.

I obfuscate.

I play loosely with the truth.

Frankly, I lie.

I'm a human being, and that makes me an automatic interpreting machine. I tell stories about my life, and most of them are only marginally connected to reality.

For most of my life, as I said in the previous chapter, I've told myself I'm not athletic. I was that kid in your gym class who was always one of the last picked for a team.

I was the kid who always got a charitable C in gym except for the one marking period in 12 years of school when we had a semester of swimming. I was a good swimmer, and I thought I was going to blow Mr. Hargraves' mind by my swimming prowess and honestly earn an A in gym. But Mr. Hargraves didn't seem to be on the same wavelength. He could only be budged as far as a B.

The prospect of physical-education-class-induced pain and humiliation held me back. Ever since I was a young squirt attending summer camp, when I found myself forced to play baseball, I couldn't help but envision myself misjudging fly balls and getting my teeth knocked out. So—being no dummy—I'd snatch the right field position. And I played it VEEERRRY deep. Any ball that managed to make it out that far was guaranteed to be a ground ball.

As a teenager, when everyone was packing their skis and heading for the slopes, I was frozen in place at home, terrified by the vision of barreling down a mountain out of control and stopping only by means of a rib-cracking thud against the side of the lodge.

At the beach or pool, I would invariably imagine myself trying to do diving tricks and, instead, cracking my head on the board or the dock.

At one point of my life, breathless from a mandatory mile run in gym class, I vowed never to run again. Even with a raging grass fire or a river of volcanic lava advancing on me, never again would I run.

I wasn't an athlete, I'd tell myself, and most everyone readily agreed . . . not too politely or empathetically, either.

Maybe, though, we were all wrong.

Learning Who We Are

Shortly after I moved to Vermont in my early 20s after finishing grad school, I met a young couple who had just moved into my apartment building, a converted old house on a side street in my new town of residence, Montpelier.

One winter Saturday, Susan, Ron, and I decided that cross-country skiing looked like it could be a lot of fun and something we might actually be able to do. The nearby Nordic trails and slopes weren't steep, and you didn't have to display your lack of prowess in front of hundreds of other people, as you would at a downhill ski area. We went to a sporting goods store and bought three sets of skis, poles, and boots, and a how-to book.

We learned to cross-country ski by having one person read at high volume the instructions for doing a technique (such as turning or stopping or racing). Then, each of us would try the move. And—do you know?—we got pretty good. Part of the reason was our equipment. The clerk at the ski store had let us three absolute novices buy the cheapest skis on the rack, which—we found out much later—were narrow, wooden, very hard-to-control *racing* skis. By the time we finished a very steep learning curve, however, we were pretty hot.

Occasionally, we'd ski on the well-groomed trails of the posh Trapp Family Lodge in Stowe. In the course of an afternoon, we'd see 50 to 100 or more people, garbed in an array of pricey Spandex and outfitted with top-of-the-line skis, sprawled flat on their butts after attempting maneuvers that didn't make it. We—including me— in our jeans and sweatshirts, would ski around them, and for the first time in my life I felt like I might have a modicum of athletic potential.

At the same time I was learning to ski, a coworker of mine at the Boston bureau of United Press International (UPI) would come up some weekends to Vermont, where I was a UPI staff writer, to take a break from the city. We'd ski, have dinner, and then go to a live music bar and dance ourselves into the floor. I, who had been profoundly disassociated from my body, discovered I could actually dance—spasmodically, I'll grant you—at least as well as I could swim and ski. I used to think that dancing was memorizing a bunch of steps, then applying them to the beat. Finally, one night I learned to let go and let the music dance *me*. I got it.

The lies I had told myself about my disconnection from my physical self—the distortions of my reality I had conjured and bought into—had robbed me of much of the fun of being in a human body. I had no idea what my athletic potential might be.

※

A few years before my Parkinson's had set in, I took a six-day workshop in the Catskill Mountains in New York that included a lot of physical challenges. Each morning before breakfast, the 100 participants gathered for 15 or 20 minutes of calisthenics, then ran. The trail was a half mile up a very steep hill, then a half mile down. The instructions were to run full-out or stop. No jogging. No walking.

The first morning, I, as usual, placed myself at the rear of the pack. Not surprisingly, my time to complete the course was mediocre, but not among the slowest.

After breakfast, we reviewed the run, and I realized that nobody had instructed us to line up according to ability, that I had only assumed that was what we were supposed to do. I decided that the next morning I would position myself in the front of the horde near the starting line. My time came in among the top 25 percent of the group. It was upsettingly clear that I had been handicapping myself all of my life, based on my own tale of athletic incompetence.

What would be my strategy for the third day?

On the afternoon of that second day while working on outdoor challenges, I experienced and was overwhelmed by the tremendous power of great coaching. I had, for the first time in my life, coaches to move me through another challenge event, a ropes course. The power of those ropes course coaches was palpable. They were completely committed to my success. Verbally, they virtually grabbed me by the chest hairs and yanked me full-speed-ahead toward some of the events that were most threatening to me.

On day 3, I decided to take advantage of the running coaches who had been positioned along the hillside trail. I expected to have to stop a couple of times along the route, but my new personal rule for the run was to stop only if I were directly in front of a coach. Through my panting, I'd bark to the coach, "GET ME MOVING! MAKE ME GO!" The coaches were surprised that I was ordering them around, but by taking control of the situation and of myself, I got my time up among the top 15 percent of the class. To this day, I can no longer tell you with certainty that I'm *not* an athlete.

Through my insights about my relationship to athletics, I've gained some very big insights that have translated to other areas of my life that were begging to be transformed . . . like my relationship to my illness.

Illness as a Life Story

The stories according to which we live—the big meaning-of-life types of stories—are typically vague. Maybe we've never noticed them. Yet, those amorphous stories are very subtly woven into the living of our lives, and they have an iron grip on us. They are stories like these: Life is scary. Life is glorious. Life is precious. My life is doomed. My home is a safe harbor. My home is a horror. I've won the lottery of life. I've been sidelined in life. I'm a success. I'm a failure. I'm sick.

" *'I'm sick'* is a story?" you may ask. Yes, it is. It's a two-word short story that labels and acts as a catalyst for the formation of many more stories as well as the emotions and consequences that arise from those stories.

If I were to ask you what your illness means, I'll bet you'd have a ready answer.

Writer Susan Sontag, in her book *Illness as Metaphor*, explored the power of stories that people make up about their illnesses. Sontag was a cancer patient in 1978 when she wrote the book, and she focused a lot of it on metaphors and myths that have surrounded cancer and tuberculosis. Those stories, those viewpoints, she contended, have added greatly to the suffering of patients and have often inhibited them from seeking proper treatment.

In years gone by, tuberculosis and cancer have provoked extreme dread. But in time, literature began to portray TB deaths as ennobling and placid, its victims made more beautiful and soulful. A lady, it was noted, would cough and leave a small rosebud of blood on her handkerchief. On the other hand, death from cancer has been portrayed as ignoble and agonizing, the victim shamed by fear and suffering.

Psychological theories of illness, Sontag said, are a powerful means of placing the blame for illness on the ill. "Nothing is more punitive," she said, "than to give a disease meaning—that meaning being invariably a moralistic one." The subjects of deepest dread—corruption, decay, weakness—are identified with the disease, and the illness becomes a metaphor. As revelations about the Watergate scandal began to snowball, for example, President Nixon, not coincidentally, was advised that there was a cancer close to the presidency . . . and it was growing. "My point is," wrote Sontag, "that illness is *not* a metaphor . . . . Illness is illness."

❋

Despite wide praise for Sontag's book, few if any of us can restrain ourselves from continually asking ourselves—not necessarily in these words—"Why did I get sick?" "What's the *real* interpretation of what's happening to me?" We seem to come back reflexively, over and over again, to the stories we've told ourselves every day, day after day. Before we know it, those interpretations get real.

What can we do about it?

We can accept the inescapability of our drive to interpret. Now, fully conscious of our interpretations, we can invent new interpretations of our illnesses that can, for instance, transform our perspective of illness as loss (of capabilities, opportunities, and relationships) to illness as gain (of possibilities heretofore never imagined).

When I was diagnosed with Parkinson's disease (PD), I went to work on a new interpretation for myself.

A Different Point of View

I started out by looking at my own chronic illness and the meanings I'd given it. I knew the first thing I had to do on my trek toward transformation was to see and understand my story, to see what was my point of view and to understand that—negative or positive—it was still a story. Is my illness elusive and hard to diagnose? Is my illness rare? Is it contagious? Is it congenital? Is it invisible and hard for others to see and acknowledge? Is it popular or unpopular? Is it obtrusive or offensive? Is it painful? Is it crippling? Is it terminal? What stories do I tell myself that leave me afraid of my illness? Am I angry at my illness? Combative? Hopeful? Despairing? Resigned? Joyful?

I had to recognize that a point of view, by its nature, can't see itself. In other words, I needed help . . . someone who would be unfailingly straightforward, who would see my story as a story as I sorted through the interpretations I'd given my illness. As I uncovered story after story, I had to let go of those stories.

Neurologists often tell us Parkies to bring along our spouse or a friend when we come for an appointment. We're notorious for not being able to trust ourselves. We lie to ourselves, about ourselves. We're very good at accommodating each change in our condition as it comes along—and they do come along . . . with threatening regularity.

When we see our neurologist, we often come with a cheery report. We want to please our doctor, and with improvements in medications and treatments, in many cases we do feel the same as always or even better, but at the same time we're getting worse. To bring about the transformation of our experience of illness, we first must develop a profound relationship with what is actually going on inside us. What sensations are we having? Pain? Twitching? Itching? Nausea? Function shutdowns?

There is also another set of sensations occurring inside of us. These sensations are the result of our *response* to our story, sensations that are inextricably linked partners with our story, responses we call worry or anger or fear that may lead to sensations such as pain in the back or neck, nausea, disruption of normal cardiac activity, or an inability to understand and coherently convey information.

Drawing distinctions between what was happening inside of me (in noncharged, body sensation terms) and my *story* about what was happening allowed me to see things in my life that were there, and perhaps always had been there, but that I had been unable to see before. Rather than being locked into a story such as that my life was over, I was able to see that my life holds new possibilities. What we make something mean—how we interpret it—often leads to misunderstandings and emotional upsets. It's very difficult—even threatening—to be open to other interpretations. But to achieve transformation, it's essential.

Here's an exercise to try:

Consider that you can *choose* to have something you *already* have, such as your illness. Even if you're a long way down the road with a chronic illness, choosing to have it gives you some power over it.

I'll explain: About a year into my new life with Parkinson's disease, I chose to have Parkinson's. I said to myself something like, "Parkinson's, I've changed my mind. Relax and unpack; you're welcome now." And from that point on my happiness has no longer been contingent on the discovery of a cure. Despite the prevailing perspective on such things, I gave myself permission to *want* my Parkinson's. As my illness has progressed, with each new development, I've rechosen to have Parkinson's. This is not to say that I've given up hoping for a cure. As a matter of fact, I've raised thousands of dollars for Parkinson's research. Right now, though, right at this precise moment, I'm fine with my illness.

The Victim's Point of View

I first recognized the predictable nature of my stories—my victim's view of life—a long and confusing decade after I left my job at a large insurance company, an environment for which I was, to put it mildly, not terribly well suited. Lord knows I *tried* to be a corporate kind of guy.

For years, my concerned and well-meaning mother had pleaded with me: "Get a good job with benefits!" Eventually, I caved in. I got a job for which I had to wear a suit every day, worked in a cubicle that was not just *any* cubicle, but an important enough cubicle to have a coat rack and an extra chair for visitors.

For four years in the mid-1980s, I wrote and edited things such as the company's annual report, executives' speeches, news releases, and the company's monthly magazine. The company was a 1,500-employee national-scope life insurance and financial services company. People told me that I worked for the best company in the state and that I had the best job at the company ("a license to prowl," as one of my predecessors put it). I got to know practically everyone in the building, and I could find out most anything about the business I wanted to know, and come and go from my cubicle pretty much as I pleased.

But I was a misfit. To begin with, I was ambivalent about being what was in reality a mouthpiece for corporate management. But because many of the good jobs in my region of Vermont were at the insurance company, and being newly separated from my first wife, shouldering the costs of renting my own place to live and helping to support our child, I leaped at the insurance company's job offer. Fitting in was additionally hard, given my discomfort with the fundamental precept of the business: to entice customers to pony up large sums of money on a bet that they were going to die sooner than company actuaries had predicted. Not surprisingly, I had an attitude. A BIG attitude.

The lion's share of my job entailed planning, writing, and editing the company's award-winning glossy monthly magazine. That big attitude of mine manifested in what was probably some weird Freudian kind of reasoning process designed to mete out retribution to my mother. Specifically, I managed to convince myself that my monthly magazine could come out basically whenever I wanted it to come out. In hopes of getting me back on schedule, from time to time my supervisor would grant me some breathing room and consent to letting me combine issues and put out, for example, a September/October issue, or a Summer Special, or a Holiday Edition. The standing joke around the department was, "Hey, Bruce! How's it coming with the February/March/April/May/June/July/August issue?"

My supervisor, a veteran of the Hartford insurance mega-industry, had moved north to Vermont to enjoy a more relaxed way of life. As much as humanly possible, he quietly suffered and abided my chronic overshooting of deadlines, to the point that his lack of success roping me in was noted in *his* annual performance review. The reviewer of my supervisor, the company's vice president of communications, one day paid a visit to my cubicle and told me to put on my overcoat . . . we were going to take a little stroll.

My work, the vice president said as we walked along the sidewalks outside of the building, was top-notch, but he made it absolutely clear that I had to get my magazine back on track or I'd be, as they put it, looking for other opportunities. I apologized and committed to once again having my monthly be a monthly. Then the vice president paused, looked at me, and asked why I was so shaken by our conversation. I explained that I felt financially cornered by my family circumstances and that, frankly, he held all of the cards in our relationship. I had no contract with the company. I had no union to come to my rescue. He could show me the door anytime he wished, I said, and I'd be on the street.

"You have total power over me," I told him.

"You give me my power," he said, not skipping a beat.

I was both incredulous and infuriated, but mindful of my economic entrapment, I contained the explosion. "Right!" I thought. "You're the vice president. You can hire and fire. You control the budget and what we say on behalf of the company and how we say it. And I give *you* your power? Come on!" I knew I was right. It took 10 years to know that I actually was very wrong.

The Destructive Nature of Victimhood

From my perspective, I was a victim. From the vice president's, I was acting like a victim, and let me tell you, I gave a convincing performance. I even convinced myself. I whined quietly. I muttered to myself that I didn't have enough support staff to do all I had to do, that I wasn't willing to lower the standards of any publication that bore my name, that I'd take the time to do my job right, that the department was in chaos and it wasn't my fault. I never knew, I fumed, when an unforeseen, disruptive "emergency top priority" project would get flung my way. I'd gripe to everyone except the person who could do something about my complaints.

Yes, I told myself, I did have options, but none of them were very good. I could try to get transferred to another department, but I already had the best job in the company. Alternatively, I could walk, although in north central Vermont there are not a lot of good public relations jobs to walk *to*.

In less than a year, though, I found out about an opening for one of those rare, good Vermont PR spots, and walk is what I did . . . *and* (surprise, surprise!) I found myself a victim at that new job, too—a righteous victim and a very unhappy one. Two years later, I walked from that job. My story about walking and the state of my life the second time around was much like my insurance company story, only bleaker, for now my short list of prospective employers had become even shorter.

❈

Over the years, I've become something of an expert about stories and the power they have over us. They often sneak up and snare us before we can even blink. Until that day with the vice president—although I had never verbalized it or even clearly thought about it—I had created the story in my head that I was something akin to a modern-day indentured servant, and short of having a money bag drop before me from an armored truck, I believed my predestined fate was a life sentence of financial insufficiency. I labored hard at being the downtrodden worker, the righteous sufferer of cruel economic injustice.

By playing the victim, by making someone else responsible for my situation, I had relinquished my power, and the cost was high. By habitually taking the nonconfrontational, comfy road, in time I became nothing more or less than the Walking Dead. I had forfeited my dreams . . . if I had been free enough to dream in the first place. I had taken leave from the realm of possibility.

Claiming Responsibility

Looking back at my corporate days, four years of believing that I was a victim took its toll. It erased from my mind any notion that there could be solutions to my complaints about the company . . . about my supervisor or the vice president or the personnel department or the senior vice president who ultimately blessed my hiring and whose bailiwick included the communications department.

If I failed to find solutions within the company for my complaints, my reasoning went, I could find a good job elsewhere. And if I couldn't do that, I could create my own means of livelihood—a business, for example, or a nonprofit that addressed something about which I cared deeply. Predictably, in no time, as a top-tier victim, I even convinced myself that if I did unearth a tantalizing job opening, I wouldn't get the spot anyhow. I had very good reasons for that conclusion:

- I was almost 40 years old, and of course, that meant I was over the hill.
- For a 40-year-old, my résumé wasn't that impressive. There were a few bright spots—United Press International staff writer, corporate public relations director, college teacher— but a lot of my jobs, I concluded, had been rinky-dink.
- I had spent most of my professional life in the rural, small-pond state of Vermont. I had never been tested in a big pond. (Given the examples of many offbeat, late-blooming Vermont entrepreneurs such as Ben Cohen and Jerry Greenfield—the two ex-hippie, multimillionaire ice cream moguls who had moved up to the Green Mountains from Long Island to make their fortunes—that rationalization for my relative unemployability was particularly specious.)

I didn't know it while I was at the insurance company, but I was as powerful as the guy working in the next cubicle over and the guy in the cubicle beyond that one and the guy whose roomier corner cubicle had walls that went up almost to the ceiling and had a door. I was even as powerful as the vice president who had a couch and two chairs and a door, and whose walls did touch the ceiling. I had the power to envision who I was and what I wanted to do; the power to engage others in my vision; the power to plan; the power to arrange the circumstances I would need to make my vision a reality; the power to dance with circumstances as they inevitably would change; the power to enlist the unshakable backing of other powerful people who would stand fast for my commitment to my visions even when my commitment would assuredly waver.

Somehow, it had never occurred to me that I had any power at all. Gravity had hold of my thoughts and unrelentingly pulled them down.

Truth be told, I actually kind of liked my victim story. It made me feel like I had just a bit more of the moral edge in life than the next person. I was an anti-hero, with an audience of one. I was downcast, stuck, uninspired, uninspiring, long-suffering, and mostly asleep . . . until I woke up and caught on about gravity's pull on my thinking, that no matter how splendid might be the story I could conceive, gravity would exert its might upon it. My story—any story—would surely backfire. It took me a precious decade to wake up and see my victim story for what it was before it completely extinguished the chance for transformation.

The vice president, it turned out, was right all along . . . and generous. He didn't have to give me a lesson so big and important that it would take a decade to digest it.

Pain: Fearing, Fighting, Surrendering

Everywhere, there is fear.

I, certainly, am not without fear.

I fear the oncoming stage of my illness when my Parkinson's medications can no longer keep pace with the increasingly rapid downward slide of my condition.

I fear choking on food and ending up with pneumonia, becoming demented, and becoming forgotten and isolated. More than anything, *I fear pain*. I tell people who say they are afraid of death that I'm not at all afraid of *being* dead. It's the possibly very painful *dying* part that has me concerned.

Living with Perpetual Pain

Just before Christmas 2006, my wife, Judith, our two adopted kids, and I moved to southernmost Mexico, to the poor, dusty, remote city of Comitán in the country's poorest state, Chiapas. Judith and I chose to live there for about four months because we knew that there would be few, if any, people who spoke English. We wanted to maximize the opportunity for our son and daughter to learn Spanish. The kids readily agreed to our plan because of its ultimate goal: to eventually cross the border into Guatemala, the kids' native country, so that Alex could meet his birth mother and sisters and Fia could meet her foster parents. We also chose Comitán because of its relative safety and its proximity to fabulous Mayan ruins and an enduring Mayan culture, particularly enticing to Alex, who is full-blooded Mayan.

Soon after we settled in, the Barragan family invited us out to the countryside for a Sunday at their mini-ranch. Dr. Raul Barragan (a very funny guy who renamed me Tomás because he couldn't pronounce Bruce) had been working with Judith to build a women's cancer screening and treatment facility at the Comitán public hospital.

At the ranch, our two families ate, laughed, shot BB guns off the cottage front porch through the rain at tin can targets nailed to trees, ate some more, and drank a fairly impressive quantity of tequila. Full of bravado, I thought I'd show off a little and jump over the low-slung hammock in the main room on the first floor. It seems to have momentarily escaped me that I have Parkinson's disease. I caught my back foot in the hammock webbing and crashed onto the cement.

The next day and each weekday morning and afternoon thereafter, as I walked Fia a half mile back and forth to school, my right leg—from my hip to my heel—hurt so much I'd have to sit down for relief almost every block. For the rest of our time in Comitán and Guatemala, I limped, winced, stretched, groaned, and found little if any relief from the hell that a damaged sciatic nerve can cause. I had never before experienced such pain, such unyielding pain.

In a weird way, it could actually have been the pain that I suspect I was subconsciously wooing in order to gain the credibility and authority I'd need to complete this book. I wanted to experience big-time pain, but only *very* briefly, for an instant. Really what I wanted was pain that qualified as big-time, but—I'm embarrassed to tell you—I didn't want big-time pain that would hurt. I realize that that's slightly contradictory, but pain can do strange things to your powers of reasoning.

A Nation of Pain Illiterates

Since my fall, it's been harder than ever to come up with anything good to say about pain.

Sure, there are the usual flimsy justifications for its existence, like the old standard that if it weren't for pain, your sleeve might catch on fire while you're cooking and you might not notice until too late.

I'd be willing to take the risk.

As for illness and pain, as I see it, there are at least two major pain problems: First, in many cases, pain—the body's warning signal—often comes too late to do much good. And second, the prolonged suffering that patients endure after pain has done its job is completely unnecessary. WE GET THE POINT!

I've learned a lot about pain since my Mexico fall. I was shocked to learn that anywhere from 15 to 30 percent of Americans have chronic or recurrent pain. For as many as a third of those people, their pain can be disabling, according to Dr. Russell Portenoy, pain specialist at New York's Beth Israel Medical Center.

Aside from hurting, pain is consuming. It devours time, thought, mobility, and productivity. And money.

In conjunction with its function of hurting, pain—in and of itself—can exact an enormous emotional toll, not only on the patient but also on family members and friends. In a 2005 *Time* magazine article, "The Right (and Wrong) Way to Treat Pain," Dr. Pamela Palmer, medical director of the pain management center at the University of California, San Francisco, says, "The anxiety, the depression, the hopelessness that come with chronic pain really all have to be addressed," as do the loss of mobility and the clumsiness, hypersensitivity to touch, and other consequences of pain that can destroy the quality of a person's life.

Alan Watts, the philosopher, has emphasized that there really is no way we can escape awareness of pain. But, in his book *The Wisdom of Insecurity*, he points out, "The human organism has the most wonderful powers of adaptation to both physical and psychological pain." The human mechanism won't work right, though, he says, if the individual continues to try to push pain away. When that happens, pain thrives.

Norman Cousins, the longtime editor of *Saturday Review* magazine and author of the 1979 classic, *Anatomy of an Illness*, contended that pain is not the ultimate enemy. "We know very little about pain," Cousins said, "and what we don't know makes it hurt all the more. Indeed, no form of illiteracy in the United States is so widespread or costly as ignorance about pain—what it is, what causes it, how to deal with it without panic."

The moment we feel pain or *fear* feeling pain, we rush to gobble down painkilling drugs. In a recent *New York Times* article, "Mind Over Matter, with Help from a Machine," pain researcher Dr. Christopher deCharms, stated that Americans spend an average of $900 a year on pain medications.

Many painkillers, warns Cousins, conceal pain without correcting the underlying condition causing the pain. The body can pay a high price for suppression of pain while ignoring its basic cause. "Most people become panicky about almost any pain," Cousins asserts. "On all sides they have been so bombarded by advertisements about pain that they take this or that analgesic at the slightest sign of an ache. We are largely illiterate about pain and so are seldom able to deal with it rationally."

One of the least-known and most important factors about

pain, Cousins says, is that approximately 90 percent of pain isn't an indication of poor health but is the result of factors over which we have some control: stress, suppressed rage, insufficient sleep, overeating, poor diet, smoking, excessive drinking, inadequate exercise, or any of the other abuses encountered by the human body in modern society.

※

There's good news on the pain front. Researchers and practicing physicians are, more and more, coming to look at serious chronic pain as not solely a side effect of illness and injury but as an illness in its own regard. Pain, we're learning, is not healthy. Chronic pain affects a person's entire body. Over time, the nervous system becomes more sensitive to pain and less receptive to the brain chemicals that moderate or turn off pain. With long-term pain, the patient's nerves may sprout sensitive new endings; receptors for natural compounds that alleviate pain may deaden; and pain mechanisms may be triggered by stimuli as mild as, say, a cool spring breeze. Eventually, the whole body may be affected if the depression and anxiety that often accompany chronic pain produce abnormal levels of certain neurotransmitters. Early treatment of physical and psychological deterioration can slow the progression of irreversible nervous system changes.

In the *Time* magazine article mentioned above Dr. Sean Mackey, director of research at the Stanford University's Pain Management Center, explains that "Pain causes a fundamental rewiring of the nervous system. Each time we feel pain there are changes that occur that tend to amplify our experience of pain." That's why, researchers say, it's a mistake to ignore or undertreat severe pain. Pain control is not a peripheral medical issue.

Many patients don't know that they don't have to suffer, that there are procedures and pharmaceuticals that can be highly effective in handling pain. Commenting in an ABC news report concerning the 2004 Joint Commission on Accreditation of Healthcare Organization's issuance of standards for addressing pain, June Dahl, a University of Wisconsin pain specialist who helped write the standards, commented, "People think it's like an 11th commandment: 'Thou had surgery, thou should have pain,' or that if you have cancer, you must have pain."

Francis, a true-blue Vermonter and a close family friend, at the age of 87 badly strained his back trying without help to lug his camper unit to a new storage spot on his property. For weeks, Francis looked miserable, so, with some effort, I talked him into seeing a doctor. The doctor, an affable fellow, greeted Francis and asked him how he was doing.

"Oh, pretty good!" Francis said. (I couldn't believe my ears.)

Then the doctor asked Francis to rate his pain from 1 to 10, with 1 being almost imperceptible and 10 being almost unbearable.

Francis thought for a minute, then said, "8."

Vermonters value pain. They seem to value it like a battle ribbon or badge of heroism. There's some kind of payoff in suffering that I don't understand.

Although medical research isn't at the point where we can eliminate all pain for all patients in all cases, much of the pain we suffer can be relieved.

A Third Way

Fighting against debilitating pain or major illness, and giving up the battle, are really two sides of the same coin. If you aren't fighting, you're looking over your shoulder to see if your adversary is advancing on you. With either option, you're never free of worry.

Another response to pain is not to be found on either side of that coin. A third way is the path of surrender, of taking the middle way, as taught in Buddhist philosophy, an approach wherein we willingly surrender our position. This provides a win–win resolution of the matter at hand. As outlandish as the notion might seem, an illness can take up lifelong residence within us or even kill us, and we can still be co-winners. We win by choosing to have the illness, by giving it permission to exist, and by mining all of the treasure of wisdom hidden within the process.

The third way isn't as popular in 21st-century America as it was during, let's say, the fifth and sixth centuries BC in the Far East. Today, many of us see the decision to not fight as giving up—a dishonorable, tragic thing to do. Skim through the family-written obituaries in your local newspaper and you're likely to find notices honoring the deceased for "fighting hard," "battling for months (or years)," and "never giving up." To surrender, to take the third way, the middle way, is akin to treason in the wars happening within our 21st-century bodies.

The third way doesn't abrogate our responsibility for maintaining the best health possible. And it doesn't mean rolling over and not being as fully involved in our lives as possible. By *surrender*, I mean something like acceptance, as Dr. Elisabeth Kübler-Ross, the author of *Death and Dying* and an authority on the human dying process, used the term *acceptance* means fully grasping the *much* bigger picture of what's happening and the truly practical approach to being with your illness: no more fighting . . . peace.

My dad died peacefully in March of 2008. He was 94 and absolutely exhausted from living, but he kept his good humor to the end. The end wasn't a sad thing for him. He was spent, and during his last month before punching out for good, he was sleeping 20 to 22 hours a day.

"The only thing I don't like about taking a nap," he grinned at me a few days before his death, "is waking up."

There's no question in my mind that he took the third way.

Stuck in the Muck

Here in Vermont, we like to say that we have five seasons—the regular four and a fifth that comes to this backwoods state between winter and spring. We call it Mud Season. Thawing snow and rain combine to turn hundreds of miles of dirt roads into chocolate pudding. Deep ruts dug by those who have gone before us snare the wheels of our cars and trucks and pull our vehicles off the road. Drivers who go too fast end up in ditches. Drivers who go too slowly lose their momentum and dig themselves into quagmires.

The paths of our lives are a lot like Vermont country roads—they are easy to traverse most of the time, and part of the time they are treacherous byways of muck.

Facing the Truth

It's easy to tell if you're stuck in the muck in Vermont, but how about *life's* muck? Here are some very good indicators that you're stuck:

When you're entrapped by unshakable negativity, you're stuck in the muck.

When life seems like nothing more than a heavy burden, you're stuck in the muck.

When nothing seems funny, you're *completely* stuck in the muck.

When you're preoccupied a lot of the time by other than what's happening *now*, you're stuck in the muck.

When you're doing things you love doing but it feels more like working than playing, you're stuck in the muck.

When other people—maybe *all* other people—come across to you as stupid or wrong and you feel that you have to argue with them or prove that you're right, you're stuck in the muck.

When you can't accept other people's sincere health tips, you're stuck.

When you argue for a point of view about which you don't really care, you're stuck in the muck.

When you're in a rotten mood because something you intended to have happen didn't, you're stuck in the muck.

When you should have communicated something but didn't, probably you're stuck in the muck.

When you can't listen, you're stuck in the muck.

When you make circumstances—and not yourself— responsible for the way your life is turning out, you're stuck in the muck.

When a dream goes unfulfilled and you get ugly about it, YOU'RE REALLY, REALLY STUCK IN DEEP MUCK!

From time to time, we all get stuck. Take my former father-in-law, Art, for example.

Art's Story

Arthur traveled cynically and with resignation through life. From his early days when he was a hard-to-control, rebellious kid to his final days lying comatose in a hospital, he was a man resigned to struggle.

Art was a Vermonter's Vermonter. My first undeniable confirmation of his genuine Green Mountain Yankee mind-set came the first winter I knew him. No matter how cold it might get, he'd wear his old, worn, thin, red plaid hunting jacket when he went outdoors . . . and no gloves, even though his hands were icy and cracked.

"Why go through a winter if you can't suffer a little, right, Art?" I kidded him.

"Yep."

A classic Vermont native, Art was a man of very few words. ("Never miss the chance to keep your mouth shut," he once told my ex-wife.)

Art was born on the family farm on a hill about 10 miles north of Montpelier. Because he wasn't the eldest son, Art didn't inherit the farm. The farm went to a brother. There wasn't much else to pass along to the rest of the offspring. Art and his wife, Kit, bought and nicely fixed up the old, rundown farmhouse down the hill from the farm, along the paved town road.

"The story of my life," Art would say, with a slight grin.

After World War II, Art got a job delivering office equipment and furniture for a local business. Years later, he bought the business, but he could never turn it into the cash cow it had been in earlier years when, among other things, it furnished the entire new headquarters of the life insurance company for which I would work many years later.

He stored his inventory in a former machine shop on the edge of town. Within a week after he significantly decreased the insurance coverage on that inventory, the building burned to the ground.

"The story of my life."

A few years later, the building in downtown Montpelier that adjoined his storefront also caught on fire, severely damaging both buildings. Guess what Art had to say about that.

Art eventually turned over his business to his son. One afternoon not long after that, Art stopped by the new office space, said he had an awful headache, went outside, lay down on the backseat of his car, and fell unconscious. He had had a ruptured cerebral aneurysm, and a few days later he died. Guess what, from the Great Beyond, he's probably *still* saying.

There was and is, of course, no *real* "story" of Art's life. Over the span of his nearly 70-year lifetime, there were, however, lots and lots of things that occurred. Art had a knack for picking out the bad things, stringing them together, and considering what he had created his life story. He had a natural proclivity for piling up evidence that his life was doomed for calamity. Inevitably, this competent, principled, funny man of good common sense would live a life infused with ample doses of disappointment, bitterness, and struggle. He gave himself little space in the story of his life for joy and success to show up.

Getting Traction—Changing the Story

Like Art, most of us create a story around our lives in order to survive emotionally, sometimes even physically. Unfortunately, these stories are almost certainly created by us not out of our enlightened and powerful vision of what we could be, but *in reaction* to things

that have already happened to us. They are created to compensate for things we perceived as lacking or wrong with ourselves . . . in a sense trapping us in the past. As we go through life, we test out different possible variations of who we think we should be. We try out different approaches to life. When a part of the story fails, we jettison it; and when one works, we use it—over and over again.
We allow it to ensnare us.

Getting unstuck means looking at how we view our life's story—whether it is ours, whether it is current, whether it will satisfy us.

Sometimes we add elements to our story that are handed to us, without even questioning them. In the realm of illness and treatment, fully entrenched story elements abound, like these old one-sentence favorites:

- Sick people are worthy of pity.
- They did it to themselves.
- A good patient follows doctors' orders.
- Pain is bad.
- No matter what, don't let a patient die or you've failed.
- Doctor knows best.

Within our stories, we create reasons for doing or not doing something and believe these reasons are true when in reality we are doing or not doing something because of other, deeper motivations. What we consider the reason we are sick or the reason we got better is just that, a reason—nothing more, nothing less. It isn't who we are or what our life story is about.

My contention is that living according to an outdated story that doesn't reflect who we are but merely lets us get by isn't living. It's surviving. Life is either a daring adventure . . . or nothing, claimed Helen Keller.

Once we realize we're stuck in a life story that is making us unhappy, we need to get help. There's no way around it. That which has us stuck has overpowered us. In most cases, the help we need to get unstuck can come from a friend, but *only* the kind of friend with enough backbone not to put up with our whining, our emotional explosions, our tears, and our unwillingness to even *look at* another point of view. We want a friend we know really cares about us, a friend who won't flinch at what will probably be our wacky reaction when she or he mirrors back to us the hard-to-bear truth about our lifetime of lying . . . our actions based on incorrect reasoning or assumptions . . . our meanness and pettiness.

To get unstuck from a deeply mired life, we need to find someone to *intrude* into our lives. We need to find an intruder who can see beyond our personalities . . . as whiners, waifs, martyrs, phony bravado types. We need to find someone who finds joy in our courage to speak the truth. We need an intruder who won't let us pile our complaints and problems onto him or her and shirk our own responsibility to resolve them.

We also need to get clear about the benefits we reap from remaining stuck in the muck versus the costs of staying stuck.

"Benefits?" you may be thinking. "*Benefits* of staying stuck?"

Yes, and there are many. One big benefit of choosing to stay stuck is that we retain our sense of entitlement to complain, as well as ownership of all of those great excuses that go with the role. We can complain about our bad luck, about how we can't do the things we want to do, about our misery. We have excellent, ready-made reasons to explain why we haven't fulfilled our dreams, why we've never reached our full potential. We hope for, frankly, a bonanza of pity.

The state of being stuck has its costs, too. It can isolate us. The great cynicism that goes hand-in-hand with being stuck keeps us ducking under the covers of life instead of finding the medical care we need and improving our well-being. I know that the overwhelming feeling of resignation that many seriously ill people feel often keeps them from doing something as simple and potentially helpful as checking out support groups, raising money for research, participating in clinical research trials, and demanding adequate treatment.

What is the ultimate cost of staying stuck in the muck? Nothing less than our lives. Staying stuck in the muck is a death sentence, the sentence of a life unrealized.

As we become clearer about what our real story is, as we see more clearly the untruths we've been telling ourselves, the easy answers we've depended on, we can figure out the sources of our thinking—what happened in our lives that led us to create a story that is keeping us unhappy. From that point, we can figure out new ways of approaching life *now*, ways that will foster our sense of freedom and vitality. Since we're all story- and excuse-generating machines and we're going to be making up stories anyhow, I suggest that we make up stories and adopt points of view that will give us support . . . legitimate, viable stories that can help make our lives what we want them to be. Believing in a different story can get us unstuck.

Once you abandon your old story, however, be forewarned that you may come face to face with one of the hardest passages in your story to give up, the passage about being a small, unimportant sick person who can't make much of a difference in the world. With the abandonment of that part of your story will come real power. It will become obvious to you that it's time to get to work.

I call on you to bravely transform your experience of chronic illness, of incurable, unpredictable, unrelenting chronic illness, and—sick or not—see that it's very possible to live a happy, exciting, and fulfilling life.

A Place of One's Own, a Place of Possibility

Many of us believe that we're living in the present, the now, but we actually are not in the real *now* at all. This place we call now, from which we steer and maneuver our thoughts and actions, is actually a place in the past.

The true place of *now* is different from other places we know. It is both a place in time and a place *not* in time.

If we actually, consciously chose to live in the place that is both in time and not in time, we would live much differently than the way we live now.

Breaking Out of the Past

Most of us construct our lives based on lessons learned in our past, which of course, makes a lot of sense. We work and build and buy and play and travel and worship and raise our kids based on what we've experienced and learned in the past. That's not a bad thing. We've learned valuable lessons in the past. We've learned a lot about how to get what we want and how to avoid making mistakes and getting hurt. We've learned how to survive. Unfortunately, we end up avoiding, repressing, fearing, regretting, and knotting up about what *might* happen based on what *has* happened in our lives. The way out of this trap is to stand firmly within our vision . . . our vision for ourselves, for our family, for our cities and towns, for our country, for our world . . . *while being grounded in the present.*

What many of us also try to do is drag our knowledge and experiences of the past into the place we call the future, which is a place—by definition—we can never reach! The future is always out there somewhere . . . never here . . . never now. Our conception of the future is, again, determined by our past.

This seldom-acknowledged, extraordinary place that's neither in the past nor in the future but that really and truly exists right now has a name: *possibility*. When we live our lives operating from possibility, we discover a new freedom. We become skilled in detaching our thoughts and actions from the enslaving power of our past.

I had never thought about possibility as a place, as a home base, before I encountered the brilliant work of Landmark Education, an international human development training organization that teaches participants to think of themselves as entities wishing to bring into reality new possibilities about which they may have only previously dreamed. These aren't projects emanating from the past. Participants create their projects anew. Participants create projects that are a direct outgrowth of the possibilities they see for their own lives and for the world.

As a Landmark participant, I had the opportunity to stand before a group of 150 people, set my old, cautious identity aside, and declare that I was a possibility—the possibility of huge numbers of people from widely diverse backgrounds coming together and finding joy and fulfillment in the process.

My declaration, I admit, was a little on the vague side! But I kept tinkering with it, trying to sharpen an idea for a course project, an event that would touch hearts, that would enable participants to experience undeniably the fundamental oneness of all people. After doing some wordsmithing, I had my project: I would invite to Vermont—at that time the whitest state in the nation—a 100-member African American inner-city gospel choir from Newark, New Jersey.

Making the Possible Reality

I had been to New Hope Baptist Church, the choir's Newark home, a few times, but this project would be brand-new turf for me—not only the gospel music part and the putting on a concert part, but the part about bringing together hundreds of people of different races and strikingly different backgrounds. Prior to the New Hope concert, I had hardly ever spoken with an African American. I grew up in Madison, Wisconsin, in the '50s and '60s, and at my 2,200-student high school, there were only two black kids. One was an AFS student from Uganda; the other, the daughter of the head of the Madison NAACP.

There's no question that my extremely limited experience made me unqualified to take on something as big as an inter-racial, inter-most-everything visit and concert involving the 100-member 11 A.M. Mass Choir, a half dozen musicians, about 700 audience members,

75 volunteers, and 50 members of the New Hope Boosters Club who came along to support the choir and to be a part of what was shaping up to be a Saturday night to remember. I had always considered myself a good number 2 or 3 person, but not a leader. Qualified or not to lead the project, I nevertheless was the guy with the vision and the guy who had to be at the helm. I dove in.

Bringing New Hope's 11 A.M. Mass Choir to Vermont and producing their concert took an enormous amount of work.

On an overcast Saturday in April of 1993, the New Hope buses rolled into Brattleboro, Vermont. We found out years later that as the buses rolled down Main Street, one very wary choir member who had been looking out the window rushed to the director and said, "They're all white! What are we going to do?"

"We're going to sing for the Lord!" said the director, the unflappable Anne Moss. And did they ever.

In an interview after the concert, Anne told a reporter, "All our hearts came together, and we were one in the spirit. If Jesus had come walking in the door, I wouldn't have been surprised."

To make my vision a reality, I had a multitude of things to do: I had to find a venue, reserve lodging for 150 people, set up a bank account and a bookkeeping system, obtain liability insurance, and have posters and tickets and programs designed and printed. (I personally put up at least 2,000 posters.) I wrote and distributed news releases and public service announcements. I did radio, TV, and print interviews. I found and rented a Hammond B3 organ. I recruited scores of volunteers. I had gift baskets with hand-written welcoming notes placed in each New Hope visitor's motel room. I arranged to have the event videotaped and broadcast over the local public access TV station. I lined up an American Sign Language interpreter for the sizable group who were students at the nearby Austine School for the Deaf. I arranged a sit-down luncheon for the New Hopers when they arrived and a free reception after the concert for everybody—choir members, boosters, helpers, audience—totaling almost 900 people so that everybody would have a chance to meet and begin to establish connections. I had a bakery make a gigantic cake for Mrs. Moss, whose birthday was that weekend. Her daughter, Felicia, who has sung and toured with her cousins Dionne Warwick and Whitney Houston, sang for her mother. I had the local select board pass a resolution declaring the weekend of the choir's visit the Weekend of New Hope.

What I *didn't* do was charge more for tickets sold at the door. As a result, I didn't have any advance idea how many people would be attending the concert. And even though the concert was a not-for-profit event, I still needed thousands of dollars up front to cover expenses. Up until about an hour before the concert, I had no idea if the event was going to be a success or a complete disaster. In rural Vermont, concerts, shows, and most other events almost never sell out. I don't think, to tell you the truth, that Vermonters would even buy a ticket in advance for the Second Coming.

As I said, I was a complete novice.

What sustained me over the year of preparation and worry was the vision of 100 radiant New Hopers, stunning in their robes, powerful, marching side by side down the three aisles of the old Brattleboro First Baptist Church, bursting with love and joy, making their way to the altar where they would let loose with their first rafter-rattling chord.

For a year, I had rigorously worked from that vision, that possibility. That possibility was so real for me, so moving that when-ever I thought about it, I choked up.

One indication of the *magnificence* of the concert was that people who couldn't be wedged inside the church that night stood outside in the rain for three hours, listening to the choir through an open window.

One indication of the *transformative power* of the concert came a year later when the 11 A.M. Mass Choir returned to Vermont, along with New Hope's senior pastor, Dr. Charles E. Thomas. Rev. Thomas hadn't come to Vermont the first year, but after hearing stories about the incredible time the choir had had, he made it the next year. About a month later, I and a few other Vermonters went to Newark for the choir's annual anniversary program. After the last song, Rev. Thomas stood at the altar, looked out over the crowd of more than a thousand people, and said, "I want to tell you, my church, about my recent experience in Vermont.

"When I was a little boy growing up in Alabama, every day I used to walk five miles to school and five miles home. As I walked along, the bus would pass me, filled with white kids leaning out the windows shouting hateful things at me. In time, I grew calluses on my feet and calluses on my heart. Now, after my recent experience in Vermont, I judge people by who they are, not what they are."

The church virtually exploded.

That moment was the culmination, the fulfillment, of all of my work to bring together, in love, people from what I call ridiculously diverse backgrounds. My possibility had become my vision, and my vision had become reality. Actually, what has come into being has been much, much greater than my vision. Many Vermonters have subsequently gone to Newark on their own. One Sunday morning in Newark, Rev. Thomas called us Vermonters "New Hope members who just happen to live in Vermont." Mom and Pop Sullivan, an elderly Newark couple, adopted my gospel-loving buddy Paul and me. Mom would get a big kick out of taking visitors to her kitchen and directing their attention to the photos on her refrigerator door, which included prominently positioned shots of her two very white sons and her five very white grandchildren.

Being the Possible

I know that the possibilities for transforming the experience of a serious, unrelenting illness are endless and can be every bit as great as the possibility I created for generating joy and fulfillment that was played out through visits to Vermont by the New Hope choir. The point isn't so much the projects or activities—the tools—that you use to bring about the essence of your vision. I could have done many other things instead of putting on concerts. The point is the greatness and profundity of what you can bring into being. The joy, itself.

As far as having Parkinson's goes, I'm the possibility that all people of the world with the disease will be able to be cured within the next decade. When I was diagnosed in 1994, I was told there would be a cure in 5 to 10 years. We didn't achieve that goal, so I'm starting over again.

I'm also the possibility that while we're waiting for that cure, those of us with Parkinson's will be able to benefit from treatments that will slow down, halt, and perhaps even reverse the course of our illness.

I'm the possibility that those of us who are disabled by our illnesses will be able to obtain a livable income and the maximum degree of independence possible.

I'm the possibility that anyone with a chronic illness can make huge, genuine contributions to others.

I'm the possibility that I can have a great life not *despite* my illness but *with* my illness.

The Heart of the Matter

This morning on the radio, as I write these words, a political journalist is reporting the good news that although the world economy is collapsing into a major international depression, it isn't collapsing as fast as it had been. People I've talked with don't seem particularly enthusiastic about this positive turn of events . . . for some good reasons.

In unprecedented numbers, many of those people are being laid off from their jobs; they are facing bankruptcy and foreclosure on their homes; they are seeing their life savings being wiped out overnight. People are weary and afraid.

"Maybe the whole point of life is to *endure* it," a generally upbeat friend said to me recently. She was making a joke, but it was a serious one.

Is there a point to going through all that we go through? What, beyond earning a paycheck (certainly an understandable goal), is the underlying point for a tragically huge number of us getting up early five mornings a week and rushing to work for 40 or 50 years of our lives? When I taught at Montpelier High School years ago, I would walk from our house to the school. I walked opposing the heavy stream of traffic pouring into the state office complex, and I made my walk into a game: How many drivers could I spot who didn't have glum, resigned expressions on their faces? On an average day, there were two or three.

Of course, for most of the people of the world, conditions are much harder. What, for those people, is the point of living a life, especially when that life is a life of poverty, famine, warfare, fire, and flood?

And I ask you, what is the point of living a life with an incurable, grave illness?

The point, I submit, has to do with a quest we're all on, a quest that's driven by an urge to know or experience something, something difficult if not impossible to identify or describe. But I'll try.

It Wasn't about the Burgers

My first conscious experience of that something came on an otherwise unremarkable Saturday morning in Madison, Wisconsin, my hometown. My buddy Lloyd and I were 11 or 12 years old, and it was the early '60s. I had spent Friday night at Lloyd's house, and early the next morning we counted what little money we had . . . just enough to cover round-trip bus fare between Lloyd's house and downtown. In a gentle drizzle we headed out to the bus stop, and in a short while the bus pulled up. The driver was pleasant but not unusually so. The route we traveled was the same one we had taken often. There was seemingly nothing special about the day. Downtown, we ambled into and out of a few stores, unable to buy anything, but as we exited a big department store (ironically advertised as "Madison's Most Interesting"), we spotted on the lobby floor one of those small, oval, squeezable rubber change holders, filled with coins. We counted them and realized we had exactly enough money to each buy a hamburger at Rennebohm's drugstore. We did, then came home.

I actually hope you've found this little story to be as dull as drugstore food. If so, I'll have succeeded. My point is that, on the surface, that Saturday morning in Madison was mundane, but the way I *experienced* that morning well over 40 years ago has been unforgettable.

I was in a charmed state that day. For hours, I experienced an unbreakable connection and synergy with the people I encountered . . . with Lloyd, with the bus driver, with the anonymous person who lost the change holder, with store clerks and shoppers, with the neighborhoods through which we rode, with everyone and everything. Even with the rain. There was a magic to that day, a dance, an all-pervasive sense of quiet yet great delight. Everyone seemed to be playing a role in the day's serenity and special happiness. I was completely filled up—that is to say, fulfilled. (By the way, I doubt to this day that Lloyd ever knew what I was experiencing. Kids don't talk about such things.)

It wasn't about the burgers. Nor was it about the bus ride or the weather or Lloyd's talent for coming up with ideas for fun things to do—or even about the coin holder we found (and, yes, in retrospect, we should have known better and turned it in to the store's lost and found). For many years, I chalked up my state of mind—and heart—that day to luck, to being in a good mood, to having had a good brain chemistry day with my endorphins a-flyin'. I longed for the next such day to make an appearance in my life, and there were a lot of great days, but none with the quality of that Saturday morning a long time ago.

Over the years, I pretty much forgot about that day. Pretty much.

Years Later, It Was about the Stars

A far more intense experience occurred a dozen years after that Saturday morning bus outing with my friend. It happened in the wee hours of a frigid winter's night in the early 1970s in my newly adopted Vermont hometown of Montpelier. An entire universe opened to me that night, and it happened in, literally, the twinkling of a moment.

It was about 2 or 3 a.m., and I was exhausted yet wide awake, my mind racing. A brisk walk around Vermont's tiny capital city, I reasoned, might sufficiently tire me so I could get some sleep. I put on my ski jacket, hat, and gloves, and outside I went. It was one of those January nights when the mercury had plunged to maybe 20 to 25 degrees below zero, so cold that the snow squeaked underfoot as I walked along. The air was still, though, and except for my face, I was warm. I had the whole town to myself as I trekked through neighborhoods brightened by electric Christmas candles that homeowners had left glowing in their windows to add a touch of warmth to the bleak post-holiday season.

Eventually, I found myself near the statehouse, Vermont's small, gold-domed, classic granite capitol building. For some reason I looked up into the deep-winter sky, and I was overwhelmed. The sky was filled with a million stars, and they all were, to me, liquid dots of color—like gemstones—lush ruby red, sapphire blue, emerald green. Then something miraculous happened. Simultaneously—*absolutely* simultaneously—I experienced me in the stars and the stars in me! The experience flipped back and forth and **BACKANDFORTHANDBACKANDFORTHANDBACKANDFORTH**. It was like standing with your back toward a mirror, trying to turn around quickly enough to be able to catch the image of your back *before* you turned. It can't be done. At the same time, neither could I separate myself from the stars.

As dramatic as my experience of oneness with the stars was, however, *the experience wasn't about the stars*. As with the bus ride years before, the experience at the statehouse was about a *feeling* . . . a feeling within me of being filled completely with a sublime happiness . . . of being fulfilled . . . filled with universal all-pervasive love. I was overcome, and I wanted that feeling never to go away, but of course, by the next day it had faded. Although I didn't realize it for a long time, on that cold night I began what would ultimately be a successful search for someone who could show me how to access and revel in that inner experience of well-being and joy.

In a Darkened Room

I remember once or twice, as a kid in my mid-teens, seriously suspecting there was something fundamental about life that I didn't know or understand and that, maybe, I *could* know and understand.

As I thought about the matter, it became pretty clear to me that if I could sit somewhere without any distraction whatsoever for a day or two, I would get the grand realization I had an inkling was out there. My bedroom would be just the right place, I reasoned, because it was somewhat isolated from other rooms in the house and it had a nurturing feeling to it . . . a good place to have this very important inner adventure. Making the room just right would require moving everything out to eliminate possible attention-diverting distractions. The hope was that, in time, my mind would completely quiet down and make way for my grand realization to occur. To prepare the way, I would cover the windows to block out as much light as possible and jack the heat up a bit so that I wouldn't eventually get too cool and have to get up and fiddle with the thermostat.

And I would take the phone off the hook.

Mainly, though, what it would take for me to have the experience I hoped to have would be for the rest of the family to be gone . . . to have the house quiet and to myself. That necessary confluence of factors never came to be, but for years I retained a vague image in my head of the basics I would need to have a setting for uninterrupted inner reflection.

Along the way on my pretty much unintended journey to discover the point of it all, I ran into a guy who lived in Cambridge, Massachusetts, who did yoga and loved it. His yoga testimonials interested me, and I decided I'd give it a try. For a year, I would wrap up work at the Montpelier UPI bureau around six o'clock and slather down a Budweiser on the way home. (It was legal at that time to drink and drive in Vermont, as long as you weren't drunk.)

I'd get home, turn on the Rolling Stones, haul out my hatha yoga illustrated how-to guide, and move from posture to posture for about 45 minutes, flipping past anything in the book that had to do with meditation, prayer, or oneness.

Like Siddhartha, the young Buddha at the river, one day, just for the heck of it, I decided to go down to the creek that ran behind the house I was renting. I sat on a big rock, closed my eyes AND PRACTICALLY WENT CRAZY! Over the years, I had thought that my always-jabbering mind was a sign of my superlative intelligence and wisdom, but in time I realized that my rushing brain was a good indicator that I was, like most everyone, more or less NUTS! Despite the nonstop yammering that was assaulting me from within, I still had a hunch that the answer to my unformed question about the point of life was, somewhere, somehow attainable.

❋

This time of my life, you should know, was not a desperate, trying, or sad time, but rather, a relatively unencumbered period of exploration, reflection, and fun. Throughout my life, I've been a basically happy guy. If something bothered me, I took care of it. My usual method was to buy a book about the issue and read it at night before going to sleep. I bought books on dispute resolution, relationships, having the perfect career, how to interpret my astrological sign, loneliness, addictive habits, winning at the game of life . . . whatever titles jumped out at me as I dowsed bookstores for convenient solutions contained between two covers. I liked to read at night in bed, but I could predictably read only four or five pages before I would get drowsy, and the new book would fall out of my hands and hit the floor. After a few days or weeks the particular problem of the moment would seem to have faded away, in time being replaced by another. My Pile o' Books, as I called it, reached an impressive height, and I could easily determine the state of my head by the depth of my pile.

I was comfortable dwelling in the safe and nonconfrontational world of type, reading to identify my problems, my shortcomings, and my woes and to find possible solutions to those matters. Deep down, though, I knew that those books would never force me to change a thing about the way I was living my life. To put my mind to rest, though, to enjoy some peace, I was sure that eventually my little backyard creek and my Pile o' Books would leave me with no need for a real, live, observant, dedicated, maybe confronting teacher.

It was at this time in my life that my friends Ron and Susan told me that they were attending small weekly programs about a teacher they said was remarkable.

"What's his name?" I asked.

"Maharaji. Guru Maharaji."

"Goo-roo? *Goooo-roooo* Maharaji? Who is this guy? What's his philosophy?"

"He doesn't really have a philosophy."

"Well, then, what's his *thing*?"

"He shows you how to have peace in your life. He gives people a practical means to connect with the peace that's already inside of themselves."

I cracked up. I'd never heard of such a thing. But I listened, nevertheless. We talked about having peace of mind, and it did sound good to me . . . a way of stopping that continual jabbering that goes on in our heads and wears us out, to say the least. I also liked the fact that the guru didn't charge anything for his teachings, that he didn't do anything to you or give you anything except a means for turning your awareness within yourself and enjoying what you find there. Unlike a philosophy, an experience was something quite tangible, something I could judge.

I was curious and also *very* skeptical. After all, at that time I had been a news writer, and the last thing an ex-UPI staffer wanted was to be suckered in by a phony guru. I had once thought that if I would ever have a mystical sort of teacher—which I was quite sure I wouldn't—the teacher I would want would be an old, white-bearded Indian guy sitting on a cushion, wearing a turban.

I listened to many people speak about Maharaji, and I concluded that either they were stark raving lunatics . . . or he was real. The speakers appeared to be telling the truth of their experience, and it sounded good.

In early December of 1974, I was shown the know-how, the simple techniques for redirecting my attention inside myself and enjoying what I find there.

Naturally, the teacher was *not* a guy with a turban but a squeaky-voiced 15-year-old Indian boy. A month earlier, I had been invited to jump into a rented van and go with about a half dozen Vermonters to Toronto to hear the boy guru speak at a large conference. I went because I wanted to see him and look into his eyes. I'd never seen a guru.

I liked what the boy—whose given name is Prem Pal Singh Rawat—told the crowd of several thousand people. He didn't claim to be the only source of the know-how to access what I call The Big It, that quiet joy that had affected me so strongly on the bus trip downtown with Lloyd, my friend, many years before as well as that freezing night in Vermont when the stars were in me and I was in the stars. He said that if you can find the know-how to unite with that joy inside of you, by all means, go and get it. But, he said, if you can't find what you want, ask him. He could help.

I figured, Why fiddle around? and I asked to be taught the know-how. I had decided that if the experience it opened up was anything like I thought it might be, it was what I had been looking for, on and off (but mostly off), consciously and subconsciously (but mostly subconsciously), for a long time. The know-how techniques were shown to me exactly 20 years before I got my Parkinson's disease diagnosis, and I want you to know that in the story of my life, the impact of this inner practice has relegated the comparative effect of my illness to a footnote.

A few words about seekers: Over the years, I've met many seekers (unlike me, *intentional* seekers) and seen many of them halt their searches. Some were afraid that in seeking the grandest of all goals, in time they would be devastatingly disappointed. Others searched and came up empty-handed because they had searched in the wrong places. They had searched outside of themselves.

Many people had continued to pursue what they'd always pursued, even though it had never fulfilled them, at least not completely. They had read, gone to workshops, acquired beautiful and inspiring things, and driven themselves to their physical limits in pursuit of a good dose of euphoria.

Like a Tuna Sandwich

I can understand if this chapter is driving you up the wall because you're reading about something that can't be put into words. I'm talking about the very real possibility of experiencing the experience that, I'll wager, most everyone has felt, probably inadvertently, at least a few times in their lives . . . the source of what

I once heard a 750-member Harlem gospel choir belt out in church-rocking song: "Joy! Unspeakable Joy!"

The best I'll be able to do is to walk you around the perimeter of the fulfillment experience. As much as I wish I could, there is no way I can satisfactorily convey through words that which is only understandable by being felt. To explain, I'll turn to my favorite food analogy, the venerable tuna sandwich.

I can describe tuna, mayonnaise, and toasted whole wheat bread. I can talk about a sandwich's taste, smell, texture, and appearance as well as its nutritional pluses and minuses. As a matter of fact, I probably can talk about a tuna sandwich from easily a dozen or more perspectives. But talk as I will, you can't *know* "tuna sandwich" until you hold one in your hands, look it over, smell its fishy/sweet smell, and eat it. Similarly, you can read this chapter and easily shut the book thinking you understand fulfillment.

But the essence of this chapter isn't in its words. It isn't in understanding. It's in experiencing the feeling that is as discernible and experience-able and practical as the eating of that tuna sandwich, only a lot more nourishing.

I don't know this for a fact (I don't think it's possible to know it for a fact), but I believe it's very likely that just about every human being, by nature of being human, is on a quest, and the irony is that we're all ultimately seeking the same thing. That which, by design, we're seeking—fulfillment—is the ultimate completing experience for a human being. We're seeking that elusive something that will make us feel *fully filled*—fully filled with happiness, with joy. Sadly, many of us, probably long ago, wrote off the notion of living a fulfilled life as an impossible delusion or the province of obscure Eastern mystics. On our quests, instead, we mostly have settled, at best, for "feeling better" practices, but not a practice that will lead us to experience The Big It.

What I'm talking about is not philosophical mumbo jumbo. It's about experiencing the *real* you inside of you. The experience that I'm talking about goes beyond what's come heretofore in this book. The experience is about an entirely new realm. In this realm, it's possible to find happiness that isn't the result of circumstances, but rather, of the fulfillment that already exists within us, waiting to be revealed. Outlandish as these assertions may seem, know that I wouldn't make them if I had not had these experiences occur in my own life. There's nothing like a major illness to put squarely before us the biggest of issues and the most challenging of questions. The introspection that grows out of the know-how reorders our priorities and lays before us new missions that may inspire us and guide us for the remainder of our lives.

While we may desperately want relief from the impact of our illnesses, while we may long for treatments that can slow, arrest, or cure our illnesses, we may find that what we want most is something about which we've thought very little. We may see that now—made vulnerable by our illnesses and acutely aware of the rapid passage of time—we are at the perfect juncture to ask ourselves some very important questions. HUGE questions, like, "Am I happy?" "Am I at peace?" are likely to arise and demand to be answered. If your answers are no, you may be compelled to ask yourself, "What's missing? What do I want? What do I *really* want?"

Here are some possibilities that you might want to ponder. Considering these possibilities will call for an open, guileless mind and heart. Thinking about them, you have nothing to lose and very much to gain.

- Consider the possibility that experiencing fulfillment is not dependent on your circumstances and good fortune. By this point in your life, you assuredly have experienced joy . . . when you fell in love, got married, became a parent, landed the perfect new job, found a great place to live. And from time to time, you've perhaps lucked out and had periodic good brain chemistry days. But you know the reality: Good brain chemistry days come and go, and happy circumstances come and go.

- Consider the possibility that the experience of that unspeakable joy, of love, is permanently within you and at all times accessible by you.

- Consider the possibility that accessing the joy within you bears a resemblance of sorts to the way San Francisco's cable car system works. The cable under the street is running all the time, and all the conductor needs to do to activate the car is to use the car's grabber device and latch onto the cable.

- Consider the possibility that there is someone, a teacher, who can show you how to latch onto your own internal joy.

- Consider the possibility that if you sincerely search, using both your head and your heart, you'll find the teacher who is best for you, someone who will show you what you're seeking, that missing piece inside of yourself.

Is it really possible to feel joy and fulfillment while living with serious, ongoing illness? My definitive answer is Yes! Not only is fulfillment possible for anyone, but it may be more probable for those who have been made more vulnerable and open through having faced disappointment and heartbreaking loss.

The power of chronic illness is that it can conquer our inertia, launching and sustaining our life's search for the experience that can make a person whole—whether seriously, protractedly sick or healthy; whether young or old; whether rich or poor.

To put it simply and straightforwardly, the point of this chapter (and this book) (and our lives), comes down to living lives of greatest happiness. Certainly not the short-term kind of crude happiness that's manufactured by theme parks or ballparks or TV and movie production companies. Not the happiness that comes from the achievement of a long-sought goal. Not even something as profound as marriage or the birth of a child or a miraculous healing. I'm talking about the kind of happiness that has nothing to do with turns of events, with circumstances, but that dwells within every human being.

Do you remain skeptical of all this? Skepticism, I acknowledge, is a reasonable response to this chapter about fulfillment . . . except that reasonableness doesn't have anything to do with the subject of fulfillment. Fulfillment is unreasonable. It's beyond reason. It's a subject of the heart.

Resolution

Amanda, who was new to the central Vermont area, had been told by a mutual friend to get in touch with me. At that time, I was in my mid-30s and single, and Amanda (not her real name) was roughly in her mid-40s, also single. I say "roughly" because I really didn't pay any attention to her age. Her age only meant something to me because it meant something to her.

Amanda was a hoot. She was brought up in a Fine Southern Family; made a big initial mistake by bonding with her Mammy instead of her Mommy; attended a respected Southern women's college; married; and took off for the West to be a hippie. But life on the vast, unpopulated western side of the Rockies was hard. Employment was meager, money was scarce, and people did a lot of waiting on tables and making of motel beds to get by. "Enough!" Amanda, in time, decided, and she called a former college friend to ask if she could make the woman's Vermont home her base of operations while she looked for a job and an apartment.

Amanda and I met for the first time for a casual dinner at a health food restaurant in Montpelier shortly after her arrival in the state.

"Amanda?" I inquired of the small, serious-looking woman sitting by the restaurant entrance. She looked up at me, broke into a warm, wide, from-the-heart smile, and with deliberateness and kindness in her voice, said, "Why, yes." I liked Amanda from the start. I liked her bronchial, no-question-that-she-thought-what-you-said-was-funny, cigarette-throated laugh. I liked her skittering nervousness. I liked her self-effacement. I liked her respectfulness.

It was fun to do things with Amanda. She was always enthusiastic and unfailingly appreciative. From time to time—every couple of months—we would go cross-country skiing, have each other over for dinner, go on hikes, sometimes take in a movie. We were two contentedly single friends who talked frankly about how we liked being single.

However, side by side with Amanda's wonderful quality of self-effacement, I would learn, was a goodly measure of low self-esteem and jealousy. Once or twice a year over the four or five years we did things together, Amanda would get furious at me, claiming that my eye had strayed toward other, younger women. As wrong as she was—and she was wrong—I would let her have her say. Invariably, a day or two later she would call me and apologize profusely for the unwarranted verbal battering she had administered. Frequently, she'd cite her abusive, now dead father, whom she'd come to hate, as the actual intended target of her attack. I'd thank her for her apology, let her cool off, and turn to a new chapter in our friendship.

One evening, out of the blue, came what would be Amanda's final attack.

At the insurance company where I was working at the time, my supervisor was the volunteer coach of the local high school boys' junior varsity basketball team. He had asked me several times to come see his guys play, so toward the end of the season, I asked Amanda if she wanted to take in a little dose of small-town life. That Friday night we went to the game. Afterward, on the way out to the car, Amanda let me have it: "I saw the way you were looking at those young high school girls! How do you think that makes *me* feel?" On and on she went.

I was dumbstruck. I had taught at the high school for four years and still knew a good half of the kids who were at the game, and it seemed like all of them stopped to say hi. I let Amanda rail and didn't address the absurdity of her accusations. But that was it, I thought, and, badly bruised, I decided to permanently cut off contact with her.

Saying What Has to Be Said

The next day while I was home the phone rang, and I let my message machine pick up the call. At work, I had all of my incoming calls screened by our office secretary. For almost a week, I let Amanda wrestle, alone, with her emotions and, I suspected, her shame and remorse, knowing that the longer I held her off, the more her feelings would intensify and the more I could punish her. Late the following Thursday night, no more than 30 seconds after I had turned off my bedside reading lamp, there was a tremendous pounding on the door of my small, isolated cabin.

I knew who was out there but was unprepared for the white-faced, bared-teeth, incensed Amanda who was on my front stoop. During the week's time between the basketball game and Amanda's late-night, 10-mile trip out to my cabin, the thought had crossed my mind that although she was slight and certainly incapable of physically overpowering me, she might be a real threat. After all, it doesn't take a heavyweight to heft a handgun.

"I WANT TO TALK TO YOU!" Amanda commanded.

"Come in," I said, shaken and nervous, realizing that opening my door may have been a very stupid thing to do. "Have a seat," I said, gesturing to a kitchen chair.

"I don't want to sit!"

"Then get out or I'm calling the state police," I said, walking to the phone.

"I'll sit," she said. And Amanda sat.

I normally can get rattled and tongue-tied in confrontational situations, but that night I knew exactly what I wanted to say. For days I had been going over and over in my head a script for a showdown, and I delivered my opening lines flawlessly and firmly. I told Amanda that she could talk as long as she wanted, but that when she was done it would be my turn. I would get equal time, and then she would have to leave. She agreed.

For 10 minutes, Amanda raged and rambled, and I sat, listening and keeping track of the time. When she stopped talking, I asked if she was done, and she started back up again. Five minutes later, she said she was finished. I asked her if she was *sure* she was finished, and she said yes. Then I made the points I wanted to make, forcefully and convincingly. I told her she had been extraordinarily abusive to me. That she had attacked me one too many times and that I had no assurance that she would stop. That she was to keep away from me at all times. I knew I had succeeded because Amanda—flushed—was silent, then looked up into my eyes and quietly apologized for what she had done. I said I forgave her . . . to please leave . . . and never contact me again.

I was proud of myself for my clarity, for my directness, and for my power. But during the following weeks my pride turned to uncertainty and then to grief. The confrontation that I thought I had handled masterfully . . . had I been out of line? Worse yet, had I been cruel and even abusive? I knew Amanda had been wrestling with gruesome psychological demons from her childhood. I asked myself if, in some subconscious way, I had been toying with her feelings of middle-aged feminine obsolescence. My questions were tearing me up. I shed tears over my confusion.

Months went by, and I begged and prayed my standard prayer for wisdom. One day, my wish was granted with a response I had not in the least anticipated.

In a way, I suppose, I had an out-of-body experience. I didn't float outside of my body, as some people say they have. It was more like a daydream. I had a perspective of standing next to the big overstuffed living room chair in which I was, at the time, sitting. I figuratively embraced myself around the shoulders and to myself thought—almost like spoken words—"Bruce, you big *schlemiel*, you may never know if you were right or wrong . . . there may not be a right or wrong . . . but you did the best you knew, and I love you." That was it. The experience, the encounter with myself, changed me. I was authentically forgiven by myself, and there arose love. For the first time in my life, I knew that I loved myself, unconditionally . . . my whole self, including (*especially* including) all the stuff I didn't like about myself.

Two years later, I unexpectedly ran into Amanda at a convention in Rome, of all places. After one of the general sessions, we went to a little restaurant for dinner, and I told her of the torment with which I had been grappling. She smiled that same warm, wide, from-the-heart smile and said, chuckling, "I thought you handled the whole thing brilliantly."

✻

My experience with Amanda gave me the strength later in my life to say what I really needed to say to someone I loved very much.

One evening in late September of 1984, the phone rang at my little cabin. I picked up the receiver and was surprised—pleasantly surprised—to hear my father's voice on the line. My mother was The Great Communicator of the family. At the slightest whim she'd call me in Vermont or my brother, Jack, in California or her relatives in Virginia. Dad would eventually get on the extension.

That September night, when I heard Dad's voice, I reflexively asked him how he was, and he said, "I'm OK, but I'm afraid your mother isn't." That afternoon, he said, a few hours earlier, Mom had had a ruptured brain aneurysm and was in a coma, dying. She would remain comatose in a Madison, Wisconsin, hospital for four days, with no apparent signs of any cognitive functioning.

Onboard the flight the next afternoon from Burlington back to Madison, I remembered what Martha, my ex-wife, had told me the year before about the hospital chaplain very strongly urging her, her sister, and her brother to each go, alone, into their comatose, dying father's room and tell him what they had to tell him.

It could not have been easy for them.

The Fitch kids were and are hard-core Vermonters, which I undeniably realized at the end of my first Fitch family event, a Christmas Eve gathering at their parents' place. Around 11, just before we all were going to head home, we gathered in a circle in the living room and opened one present each. When Martha and I got back to our apartment, I told her I knew her family didn't believe in sending thank-you notes, but, I added, "You guys didn't even SAY thank you!

Came Martha's immediate explanation: "We all knew we were appreciative. To have said thanks to each other would have been redundant."

The Fitches took the chaplain's advice, though, and found a great sense of relief and release.

My plane landed in Madison, and I caught myself thinking and, yes, praying, "Please let Mom be alive." Dad was standing at the gate, and the first thing he said was, "Let's get your suitcase and get over to the hospital." That was exactly what I wanted to hear. Years before . . . somewhere along the line . . . someone had told me that people in a coma can hear you, even though they show no outward signs of awareness. I was doubtful, but I decided that I was going to proceed like a believer. At the hospital, I told Mom just two things: "Thank you for everything you've done for me," and "I love you."

The fourth night of her coma, Dad and I saw Mom, then went home, said goodnight, and dozed off. Shortly before midnight the phone rang. It was, of course, the hospital, notifying us as we had requested that Mom had died. Dad and I dressed and drove downtown. When we walked into the room, the woman in the bed looked absolutely at peace.

I left the hospital complete with my mother that last night of her life. I had told her the two things I wanted to tell her, said goodbye, and left knowing that I loved her and that she knew it. And I knew that she loved me, and that she knew that I knew. What more was there to say or do? We both could let go.

Tying Up the Loose Ends

Part of the standard package of features that comes with each new human being is a component within us that can experience enormous satisfaction when we take care of unfinished business, when we tie up the loose ends of our lives.

There's something about that feeling. Sure, tying up any loose ends of your life feels good. There is, for example, a feeling you get when you've cleaned out the garage; and then there's the feeling you get when you say the final words you'll ever say to your mother.

It's strange and tragic that many of us assiduously avoid doing the work necessary to be complete. We tell ourselves that the task is too big and we don't even know where to start. We tell ourselves that taking care of unfinished business will be messy or scary, that things are OK the way they are. Still, that unfinished business keeps tugging at our sleeve.

Tying up the loose ends of life, or completing, is about healing relationships with the people who are important in our lives.

Healing a relationship means telling somebody something important that you haven't told him or her. The beginning of those conversations might start with phrases like these:

> *I'm angry at you . . . .*
> *Why did you . . . ?*
> *I felt hurt when you . . . .*
> *I never told you that.*
> *I'm sorry that I . . . .*
> *I care about you.*
> ...and the most important of all: *I love you.*

Not communicating what we need to communicate forces us to be guarded, to not be fully present with those about whom we care so much. To be completely open and free with others, we may have to give up a lot of things to which we may be attached: our pride, our resentments, our anger, our annoyance. We may have to give up our stake in always being right and others being wrong. We may have to give up martyrdom.

Our days and hours may be numbered, but the possibility that we can bring our life to a satisfying finale exists, nonetheless. Dame Cicely Saunders, the founder of modern-day hospice, was appalled by the deplorable care the indigent of London's slums had been getting in the last days of their lives. In the mid-1960s, Dame Cicely opened St. Christopher's Hospice. She put the patient at the heart of the decision-making care team.

The same goes today for dying patients in hospice programs all over the world. Patients want meaning, poignancy, and contentment when they die. Most want to die at home, and that can happen thanks to the advent of mobile care teams of physicians and nurses, aides, social workers, bereavement counselors, clergy, and volunteers, who do housekeeping, run errands, fetch prescriptions, give respite to caregivers, care for children, fix meals, read to patients, write letters, and do countless other much-appreciated tasks.

"Most of all," says a Vermont hospice staff member, "we listen. We're there. People who ask hospice for help don't sit around thinking about dying. They want to take care of their affairs—practical things and things going on inside of themselves. Once they're done, they're at such peace."

Dancing in the Face of Death

I'm not particularly morbid, but I love to tell the story of a poor, rural, 36-year-old Vermont woman named Linda who was dying in her shingled, falling-down house in the small, somewhat bedraggled village of Plainfield.

"We asked Linda what she wanted," said Diana Peirce, the director of a regional Vermont hospice program. "She looked right in my eyes with her big green eyes and said, 'Well, I've always wanted to meet Larry Bird.'" Hospice wrote to the Boston Celtics legend, and he sent Linda an autographed ball and an autographed picture. He also phoned her.

"What else?" Linda was asked.

Well, she said haltingly, she had, um, always wanted to go to Hawaii.

Hospice told her that the money wasn't exactly in the budget.

"Her chances were not good!" cackled Ginny Fry, the local hospice bereavement coordinator and also, conveniently, a practicing artist. With a stroke of brilliant playfulness, Diana asked Ginny if she could concoct a Hawaiian vacation for Linda, who had never been more than a few miles from Plainfield. Ginny decorated Linda's dilapidated house with fake palm trees and parrots while tiki torches rammed into the snowbanks burned outside. Linda draped a lei around the neck of each of her 40 arriving guests who had taunted frostbite by showing up wearing shorts. She gave each a big kiss. Linda had confided that she had never had fresh flowers, so hospice had an orchid lei flown in from Hawaii just for her.

To capture the smell of Hawaii, Ginny brought along a big pump bottle of coconut oil and ordered everyone to grease up. From a VCR came the sound of crashing island waves. But, Ginny said, she couldn't figure out how to make the house feel like Hawaii. Someone eventually had a brainstorm. They would turn Linda's living room into a beach. A hospice staffer got a couple of bags of driveway sand and baked it in her oven, then put heating pads and bed sheets on Linda's floor and poured the sand on top. Voila! Waikiki!

Linda did the hula.

"Linda had the chance to say goodbye to everyone," Ginny said. "She watched the video of the party every day until she died of cancer a month later. She called the luau 'My Night.' She said it was the best night of her life."

❋

The completion of a life, the resolution of a life, of course, isn't always neat and tidy like the dimly lit deathbed scenes in saccharin Hollywood film classics, where the ailing protagonist gently turns his or her head to the side, the music volume cranks up, the lighting does a slow fade. Hollywood ending or not, we still can close out our untidy lives contentedly.

Comedian Gilda Radner of *Saturday Night Live* fame wrote in her book *It's Always Something* about her ultimately fatal struggle with ovarian cancer: "I wanted a perfect ending. Now I've learned, the hard way, that some poems don't rhyme, and some stories don't have a clear beginning, middle and end.

"Life is about not knowing, having to change, taking the moment and making the best of it, without knowing what's going to happen next . . . ."

The nature of life, she eventually concluded, is a "delicious ambiguity."

The Mule, the Well, and the Power of Persistence

There once was a farmer who owned an old mule that fell into his well. The farmer heard the mule braying, but after carefully assessing the situation, he decided that neither the mule nor the well was worth the trouble of saving. Instead, he called his neighbors together and told them what had happened, then enlisted their help to haul dirt to bury the old mule in the well and put him out of his misery.

Initially, the old mule was hysterical when the dirt started to fall. But as the farmer and his neighbors continued shoveling, every time a shovel load of dirt landed on his back, he shook it off and stepped up. And this he did, blow after blow. No matter how painful the blows or how distressing the situation seemed, the old mule fought off panic and just kept right on shaking off the dirt and stepping up.

It wasn't long before the old mule, battered and exhausted, stepped triumphantly over the top edge of the well. What seemed like the thing that would bury him actually saved him . . . all because of the manner in which he handled his adversity.

That was persistence! That also was commitment, in its most basic form. The mule couldn't verbalize his commitment the way a human being can, but he was fully committed to the most fundamental commitment of all . . . to staying alive.

Staying with It

Commitment is the key secret ingredient that turns visions into realities.

Commitment. I don't know about you, but I don't even like to say the C Word.

C-C-C-Commitment. I can barely get it off my tongue.

To me, commitment often feels like responsibility. What it *doesn't* feel like is something freeing. We try hard to avoid commitments, but try as we might, from time to time, even the biggest holdouts among us have made at least one major commitment in their lives—they've committed to not having any commitments. When commitment feels like drudgery, we are at a stage in the transformational process in which we need help . . . from someone who is probably more committed to seeing us fulfill our commitments than we are. When we're ready to give up, that person can restart us and keep us going until we reach the finish line. One of my most important coaches is my neurologist, Dr. Robert Hamill. It's probably not surprising that he's my coach. Not only is he a fabulous physician, but he was also an excellent athlete who originally wanted to be a professional soccer player. But he was too small and, instead, went to medical school and eventually became chairman of the University of Vermont Department of Neurology.

Looking back to the mid-1970s when my first wife, Martha, and I were married, you can be sure that when we wrote the vows for our ceremony we didn't include the C Word . . . *anywhere*. We had gone through the '60s and the upheavals of the Vietnam War and that era's cultural revolution. We went into our marriage cynical about government intrusion into private lives, which was how we regarded state-required marriage licensing and a legally required commitment on our part. In my work in journalism, I learned to "write around" holes in stories—missing information—in such a way that readers never would catch on that there were gaps in my articles. Martha and I wrote around the issue of commitment in our vows.

You can be doubly sure that after having discovered the magic and power of the C Word, my second wife, Judith, and I practically based our entire wedding service around that word that is so disliked but REALLY DOES WORK.

Here's what a commitment can *do*: It can take an idea and transform it into reality.

Here's what a commitment *is*: A commitment is doing what you say you'll do. (Think of a commitment as the little brother of a promise.)

And here's the secret of making a commitment *work*: A deadline. If, say, I commit to volunteering at my local free clinic, that's nice. But so what? On the other hand, if I commit to volunteering at the clinic by the end of the week, doesn't that feel different? Scary maybe? Exciting? Motivating?

Judith and I had known each other for almost a year when we traveled to Guatemala together to meet Alex, the baby boy we would be adopting. From the time of his birth, Judith said it was killing her to be apart from her baby. I said to go. She said it might cost her the executive job she held. I said, "Go! You'll never regret it." So, to Guatemala we went. I stayed 10 days to help Judith get situated for the long wait until she could bring Alex to the U.S.

About five months later, she and the baby made it back, and that's when the serious phase of our courtship began. That's when our search for fatal flaws also began, with questions mostly unexpressed and mostly directed at ourselves like, "What's the real story here?" and, "What should I know that I don't know?" In short order, it became obvious that we were on a grim, destructive track. One Sunday afternoon we were driving around southern Vermont looking—for possible future reference—for a wedding reception site. I pointed out that we were putting ourselves through the heavy-duty ambivalence of trying to create a strong relationship while looking zealously for each other's flaws.

"We're human beings, for God's sake!" I blurted out. I said that we should go ahead and get married with the understanding that we both were not perfect and that we both were going to find imperfections in each other. We'd make our marriage work, and we have. (A few months ago, Judith and I celebrated our 16th anniversary, and yes, there have been some bumps and potholes as we've gone down the pike. We haven't swerved around them.)

For Judith and me, our commitment is to *have* commitments.

Since I've known her, Judith has done a lot of work for women and families. She served as the executive director of the Vermont Commission on Women; helped build a women's cancer screening and treatment clinic in rural southern Mexico; traveled to Reggio Emilia, Italy, to study a remarkable citywide preschool education program; wrote a section of a book on women and adoption; facilitated adoptions; and done research in support of the state's battered women's services. And the list goes on and on. For what will probably be the last phase of her career, Judith wants to go abroad and work with poor women and families in the Third World.

Judith and I are big talkers about helping bring about national and international peace, justice, and overall well-being. We also believe in that age-old saying that the world is reflected in a single drop of water. If we don't have peace, goodwill, and love at home, in our personal relationships, how could we ever *think* we could bring it about on a worldwide level? Learning about the distinction of commitment has not only helped us considerably in our marriage and parenting; it has also prepared us for the kind of dedication that meaningful development work abroad will require.

Illness and Commitment

Chronic illness has forced me to redefine my own mission, to let go, to ask myself what makes a person whole and productive and fulfilled. It's forced me to make new commitments.

My father, who had been an internist, saw thousands of sick people during his lengthy medical career. Soon after my Parkinson's diagnosis he told me, "Don't identify yourself as your illness." I *have* Parkinson's. I am *not* Parkinson's. That distinction has served me well.

Following Dad's advice, I haven't defined myself by my health status. But in the America of the 2000s, I've had a hard time resisting the compulsion to define myself by what I *do*. No longer can I do easily what I used to do well, and that's writing, or more precisely, the mechanical function of typing. I used to write for and edit newspapers and magazines, whacking away at keyboards at the fairly respectable rate of 75 or 80 words a minute. Someone would shout, "Talbot, I need a new lead for that story. NOW!" And NOW is when I would have it done. I simply can't do things like that anymore. With the help of a voice-activated computer system, I can generate material, but it's slow going.

I spend my days primarily as a househusband . . . a pretty unimpressive househusband. It takes, I figure, two to three times longer to do things than it used to—cleaning the kitchen, doing the laundry, shopping for groceries, fixing dinner. I try to squeeze in some freelance writing and public relations consulting, but if you figure that basic household chores take at least twice as long to accomplish, that leaves half the time that would have been available for producing income (again, at half the old speed). Unless you're writing best-selling haiku, where does that put you?

I've had many new and different commitments in my life since my diagnosis.

During the first year after being diagnosed with Parkinson's, I made the lofty declaration that my disease was somehow going to be a contribution to humankind; however, being a reasonably normal individual, I did nothing much at all for anyone. I didn't know what to do. I didn't know what I still had to offer.

Then, one day, looking in the mirror, I realized I could offer . . . my hair! Although my posture is stooped and I have the geriatric shuffle, I still have all my hair, and almost all of it is still dark brown. My thinking was that I could provide shock value for the struggle to dispel the perception of Parkinson's as an aggravating but minor disease of the elderly. My first effort at challenging the PD stereotype was to help a nearby Parkinson's support group hand out free coffee and baked goodies to fall foliage leaf peepers at an interstate rest stop. When I was introduced to tourists as a Parky, they were more than a little astonished.

Eight times so far I've lent the youth that my hair represents to a national walk in Central Park to raise awareness and research money. I've been to Capitol Hill three times to help raise awareness and the really big bucks that the federal government could be contributing for intensive Parkinson's research. I'm currently a member of the national patient advisory council of the New York–based Parkinson's Disease Foundation. I'm a trustee of the Vermont Chapter of the American Parkinson Disease Association, and I've served as newsletter editor, secretary, vice president, and president. I've participated in clinical studies and started a statewide support group for young people with Parkinson's. I've written articles and I've written this book.

It's not that I've contributed so much to the world because of my Parkinson's, but I am doing something . . . I'm fulfilling my commitments . . . and I say that not to score any accolades. By getting out of my chair, I've learned a few lessons. I've learned that putting words into action changes my chemistry. By melding my life into something bigger than my own life, I become bigger and my complaints become smaller. I get swept along.

As with the mule, if we face our problems and respond to them positively, refusing to give in to panic, bitterness, or self-pity, the adversities that come along to bury us have within them the potential to benefit and fulfill us. Certainly, such was the case with the mule. Such is the case with the chronically ill. Commitment has a bad reputation, but it works.

A Time for Hoping

I've done a whole lot of hoping over the past 15 or so years.

Since my Parkinson's diagnosis, I've been in a steady, low-grade state of hopefulness. In my mind there's a continuous, quiet hum of hoping going on that a way will soon be found to slow down, stop, and even reverse the worsening impact of my illness. In the spring of 2004, that hum of hopefulness became a thunderous cacophony of terror. The terror wasn't due to the phone call I got one morning in late May from my urologist, informing me that my recent prostate biopsy had tested positive for early-stage cancer. I was, actually, almost cavalier about the diagnosis. I had pretty much expected it; and prostate cancer, I knew, is generally slow growing and treatable. Plus, my doctor had emphasized that we had caught the cancer *"very, very, very, very* early." (Four *verys*. Believe me . . . I counted.)

I began unraveling when he told me he had already gone ahead and scheduled me for a full-body bone scan at the local hospital. His concern and sense of urgency about the possible spread of my cancer brought home to me the real possibility that I might be dealing with a lot more serious of an illness than I had initially thought.

I became *completely* unraveled when I returned home from the scan and found the message already waiting on our answering system that the radiologist had identified two suspicious, potentially malignant spots—one in my skull, the other in my left femur—and wanted to get more X-rays to determine whether my cancer had metastasized. Truthfully, I felt like I might vomit. More than anything, I felt . . . sad.

Several days later, I returned to the radiology department where I sat with my head pressed against a hard, flat, vertical surface, then lay motionless on a hard, flat table while the X-ray technicians, safely holed up in the adjoining control room, took what seemed like dozens of head and thigh close-ups.

When the session was done, I shuffled back to the patient dressing room, and for the next 10 or 15 minutes I fumbled with my anxiety-exacerbated, trembling, uncooperative, Parkinson's-stiffened left hand and leg in order to get back into my street clothes. Finally done, I stepped into the corridor and heard a fateful-sounding voice calling my name. When I looked up, the nurse said to me in a no-nonsense way, "The radiologist wants to see you in his office." There I was, alone, feeling very small, ready to get what might be the most ominous news of my life. I entered tentatively, looked around, and was staggered by the wall of back-lit films of *me*.

"Everything looks fine," the radiologist said.

I hugged him.

For the first time in what seemed like months but had been only days since my urologist's biopsy call, I *felt* hope. I emphasize: I felt hope. I grinned reflexively. I think I skipped (as well as a guy with Parkinson's disease can skip) out of the hospital and across the parking lot. I felt like I had abruptly dropped 25 or 30 pounds of weight that I had been shouldering. My stress-induced tremor calmed down.

✻

That morning at the Central Vermont Medical Center, I realized some things about hope. I realized that unlike the way most of us think of it, *hope* isn't the same as wish. Hope—true hope—is something far more tangible and powerful than a wish. I also saw that hope tends to occur on its own accord. To some degree, it's an involuntary thing . . . triggered by our emotional responses to compelling, deeply seated notions about life and, especially, mortality.

When we do what we typically consider to be hoping, it may look something like this: "I hope I can get an appointment with Dr. Jones this afternoon." Or, "I hope my chest pain is nothing serious." Or, "I hope the surgeon gets all of my tumor."

If we were asked to identify the *hope* in these sentences, most of us would say the obvious: "that I get the appointment, that my chest pain isn't serious, and that the surgeon gets everything."

Those responses would seem to be right, but I disagree . . . at least in the context of this discussion. As I said earlier, hope is not the same as wish. Hope is a feeling that spontaneously arises from wishing, the first step in the birthing of the feeling of hope.

The hope I'm talking about is not the childlike *I hope! I hope! I hope! I hope! PLEASEPLEASEPLEASE . . . PUHLEEEEEEESE!* kind of hope.

Neither is it the not-a-chance-in-the-world, longer-than-longest-shot kind of hope.

Nor is it the queasy-in-your-stomach-because-you-know-you-don't-really-feel-it kind of hope.

I'm talking about the kind of hope that goes beyond ordinary definitions of the term, such as to wish, to desire, to expect, and to anticipate. I prefer the definition of hope used by Harvard's Dr. Jerome Groopman, who also serves as chief of experimental medicine at the Beth Israel Deaconess Medical Center in Boston. In his book *The Anatomy of Hope: How People Prevail in the Face of Illness*, Dr. Groopman writes, "Hope is the elevating feeling we experience when we see—in the mind's eye—a path to a better future." True hope, he says, "acknowledges and includes the significant obstacles that we will encounter." True hope, says Dr. Groopman, has no room for delusion. He also notes that many people confuse hope with optimism. Optimism, he says, is a prevailing attitude that things will turn out for the best. Hope differs from optimism in that it doesn't arise from positive thinking or from an overly rosy forecast. Hope is rooted in "unalloyed reality."

Delusion and Truth

As a kid—like most kids—I loved TV cartoons. My favorites were those in which one character, the prankster (like that beep-beeping Road Runner) would invariably outwit, outrun, and outrage his perpetually vengeance-seeking victim (like Wile E. Coyote). I would get my biggest charge from chase scenes, especially those involving stairs.

After 45 or 50 years, my memory is a little hazy, but I have a murky recollection of a particular scene in which the Road Runner, standing at the top of a staircase, taunts the thwarted, humiliated, frustrated, and beleaguered coyote, who is hopping mad at the foot of the stairs. The coyote revs up his legs, generates swirls of dust, and rises straight up to the height of the second-floor landing where the Road Runner waits. Of course, Wile E. Coyote never reaches the Road Runner because he never zooms forward through the air to the landing as he had, cartoon-like, expected he could. Instead, he ingloriously crashes to the living room floor.

Like Wile E. Coyote, we delude ourselves with cartoon thinking that we're at the top of the stairs, so to speak, and that our hopes will, in a cartoon-like way, become reality. And like the coyote, we're highly unlikely to get where we want to go by such cartoon thinking. We need to acknowledge where we are on life's staircase in terms of our chronic illnesses and our experience of our illnesses. To have hope based on anything other than the reality of which step we're on is a delusion. That isn't hoping. It's false hoping, and false hoping is a lot like being 8 or 10 feet up in the air and thinking we're standing solidly on the stairs. We need our stair-climbing, our hoping, to be based on reality to have the traction we need to get where we want to go. False hope is hope based on exaggeration and a wish for unrealistic outcomes. To clear the way for the experience—the power—of hopefulness to come into our illness-beset lives, we must keep our feet planted on life's stairs and keep climbing, step by step. My step-by-step, reality-based progression toward true hopefulness has looked something like this:

- I've extensively researched my illness. I've become something of an expert on its possible cause, course, and treatment.
- I've fielded an outstanding team of medical care providers as well as others to provide physical and emotional support.
- Over the years, I've drawn up a number of wildly diverse treatment plans. If it looks like the end is not too far down the road, I'll also write a pain-tempering palliative care plan.
- Most important, I've put my plans into action.

At this level of clarity in my step-by-step progression—and probably not much before—I began to determine what I could hope for. Would I aim for things that may be almost certainly beyond my grasp? I don't think that there's anything wrong with having high hopes. I have a few of them, and miracles have been known to happen. But I suggest that you include hopes that have a great probability of fulfillment. Our automatic inclination, of course, is to hope the Big Hope, to hope for a cure. But we need to also look inside ourselves for other things to hope for.

You might hope, for instance, to have your illness serve some bigger purpose. There are people, including dying people, with hopes that are profound and, thus, for them, comforting, inspiring, and quality-of-life-sustaining. Some strive to be role models or poignant symbols who will help speed the way to a cure.

We can have hopes that can be realized no matter what happens to our health or our circumstances . . . hopes that, when they come to pass, leave the door open for more trust of our own capabilities and the course of our life. We can have ever-greater, ever-more-selfless hopes. A hope that occurred to me when I was told my prostate cancer may have metastasized was: "No matter what the course of my illness may be, my hope is that when all is said and done it will have been worth it." We can cultivate genuine hope even when we are acutely aware that things are not going well and the likelihood of a good outcome is small. Hope is an ongoing choice.

Hope has a strong scientific component. Some researchers believe that hoping alters brain neurochemistry. Studies have shown that belief and expectation can actually block pain by releasing the brain's endorphins and enkephalins, mimicking the effects of morphine. With hope—*true* hope—there also is an accompanying sharp upward shift in mood, like what happened in me the day the radiologist told me my cancer had not metastasized. From a medical standpoint, clear-eyed hope gives patients the courage to confront circumstances and the capacity to surmount them. Hope tempers fear so we can think, decide, and act. Hope is at the very heart of healing.

※

Be forewarned, though, that giving false hope is seductive, especially to the person who bears the responsibility of delivering less-than-ideal news. False hope is only a temporarily satisfying illusion, a lie that cannot forever be kept secret. The cost of false hope is the loss of trust. False hope paves the way for hopelessness; and hopelessness, at its most extreme, leads to despair, to being overcome by a sense of futility or defeat.

The consequence of despair, according to Dr. Elisabeth Kübler-Ross, the death and dying expert, is that everyone loses. If cancer patients, for example, come to see their condition as hopeless, the almost inevitable reaction of the patients and their doctors will be, "What's the use? There's nothing we can do, anyway." That will be the beginning of a difficult time for those patients and for those around them. The patients, Dr. Kübler-Ross says, will feel increasing isolation, the loss of interest on the part of their doctors, and greater hopelessness. They may rapidly deteriorate or fall into a deep depression from which they may not emerge unless someone is able to give them a sense of real hope.

Giving hope is something that hospice programs do extremely well. Hospice patients know they are terminally ill, yet they die with hope. They know their affairs are in order, and they know they've completed everything they needed to complete with the people they care about. They know their lives have mattered.

With despair, there is an utter lack of hope as well as a discernible, almost tangible associated emotional state. Despair is often our automatic mood default setting. Many of us—not just the seriously ill—are living Thoreau's "lives of quiet desperation." Still, with knowledge, honesty, and support, we have a large degree of control over our thoughts and, hence, over our experience of life . . . and by extension, over our lives. We have the choice to build a solid foundation of reality to support hopefulness. That firms up our hope, enabling us to withstand the unsettled weather of chronic illness and give ourselves a basis for courage and resilience.

Hope, Healing, and the Third Way

We tend to think that in regard to hoping, it all comes down to an either/or choice: To hope or not to hope (or at its most extreme: To hope or to despair). But that's not the way it has to be. With hope, there is a place—a Buddhist-type third way—where both truth and hope can—and *must*—exist simultaneously, not as jumbled confusion but as a viable way to live with illness.

Today's medical and nursing students are taught to tell patients the truth about their cases and not to string them along with fantasies. In the case of a mortally ill patient, the only treatment available might be palliative care; but even that level of care can open up precious possibilities . . . of dying among loved ones, at home, with dignity and optimum comfort management. Hope can exist even for the dying. It exists for everybody.

Although difficult to grasp, impossible to see, and challenging simply to define, we know that hope is real. We feel it unmistakably doing its work. The poet Emily Dickinson tried with verse to capture the elusive essence of hope. I think she succeeded.

> Hope is the thing with feathers
> That perches in the soul
> And sings the tune without the words
> And never stops at all.

A Time for Praying

Do I pray? Yes, from time to time I toss one out there. I'm embarrassed to admit that I mainly do it in times of crisis—personal or otherwise.

Where do I direct my prayers? Knowing that I don't know what's going on and who, if anyone or anything, is in charge on some higher level, I just shoot those rare prayers out there and wait to see what happens. Out there, I reason, there may be merely big clods of planetary dust and strange gases floating around in a tremendous void. There may be an unimaginably enormous sea of pure energy. Maybe there's an overpowering white light. Maybe our elders are out there in spirit form hoping to help us. I simply don't know. I also don't know that there's *not* someone or something out there. Like extraterrestrial-seeking astronomers who broadcast messages into deep outer space hoping for a response, I send my messages out there, too, to Whomever or Whatever may be listening.

What do I pray for?

What I pray for these days is much different from what I used to pray for, thanks to a large degree to the visit I paid quite a few years ago to Canaan Baptist Church of Christ in Harlem. That Sunday, the church was in the middle of a capital construction fundraising campaign to expand its educational wing. Senior pastor Wyatt Tee Walker, former chief of staff to the Rev. Martin Luther King Jr., spent much of his sermon that morning talking about money. At one point, Rev. Walker said something that has stuck with me for 20-some years. He said not to use prayer like a credit card. I interpret that as meaning, Don't pray for a big lottery win, a fur coat, a promotion, a date with someone who's caught your eye. And tempting though it may be, don't even pray for things for others . . . not even for unselfish good things such as your child's success in school or the healing of a sick spouse or parents. Those prayers—including the selfless ones—seem to me to be out of place when having a talk with an all-wise God.

What's left to pray for, then? I do have one basic prayer that I feel OK praying. In one of those times of crisis, when I'm silently shouting out to Whomever or Whatever, I rarely ask for a particular outcome. I ask Anybody or Anything Listening for the clarity to see what would be the wise thing for me to do and the courage and the strength to do it. For someone who knows he doesn't know, the prayer feels respectful, honest, unselfish, and for the greater good.

Aunt Harriet's Entreaties to the Lord

My Aunt Harriet, Dad's sister who is now also deceased, was a modest, dignified Midwestern woman who worked for many years as a high school and college science teacher. She wasn't the kind to make a big display of her love for the Lord. She regularly went to church but didn't attend to be seen or to score points with the Almighty. She went to church, gave generously when the plate was passed, and had, through heartfelt, consistent prayer, an always-available, comforting relationship with God. The Lord was her friend and her closest confidant throughout most of her life . . . but all that changed. During the last several years of her life, Aunt Harriet was mightily miffed at the Lord. Why, she would whisper in her barely audible voice, would God cripple and degrade her so terribly?

As an elderly woman, Aunt Harriet, like me, had Parkinson's disease. She had her share of symptoms, but the one that really bothered her was her overproduction of (or inability to swallow) saliva. She chewed gum obsessively in a futile attempt to absorb the excess, and she continually dabbed at her lips with a handkerchief or napkin to blot up the overflow. The problem drove her to distraction, and she angrily blamed God for making her life miserable and an embarrassment. Why, she pondered, would a loving God do such a thing?

Over time, Aunt Harriet's sorrowful frustrations have prompted my contemplation of some fundamental questions:

- First, the big one: Is there a God, and if so, how can a person be sure?
- Operating for the time being from a perspective that there is a God, did God have it in for Aunt Harriet? Was Aunt Harriet's illness God's will? Or was God—in a tough-love kind of way—trying to teach Aunt Harriet some type of lesson? If so, what was it, and did she get it?

- Again, operating from a perspective that there is a God, does God even *think* the same way and along the same lines as Aunt Harriet thought (or any other human being thinks), and while we're at it, does God *communicate* as human beings communicate?

My answer to all of these questions is: I don't know, and I don't think I ever will know. That perspective of not knowing, however, has proved to be a fertile place from which to face these and other matters of spirituality and its connection with the world of illness.

❋

Realizing that the subject of this chapter runs deep and is a potential theological and political minefield, I want to make it clear from the outset that I do not see it as my mission to argue theological questions or to promote a certain point of view. My intention is to present thoughts on the interplay of religion and chronic illness that may deepen the transformation of your experience of long-term, serious illness.

For countless believers, study and practice of a religious faith has no doubt deepened and accelerated in the face of chronic illness, providing solace and hope. For "not sures" and "sure there are nots," be confident that I'm not recruiting for lost souls. My purpose is to present material that will—whatever may be your relationship to matters of spirituality and faith—strengthen you and enrich you.

The following story is told in journalist Mort Kondracke's book *Saving Milly* and is a good example of how many of us sway back and forth in our spiritual relationships and how these relationships are uniquely our own to shape.

As her insidious case of Parkinson's Plus worsened, Milly Kondracke could barely eat. She was nearly unable to speak or to swallow anything . . . food, liquids, or medicine. "I feel abandoned by God," Milly, at one point, whispered to her husband, "I feel like Job."

The life-or-death decision about whether to insert a feeding tube was inescapably before Milly and Mort. Milly had vowed not to accept a tube and, rather, starve to death, and she had included the wish in her living will. But when her condition deteriorated to the point that the feeding tube issue was unavoidable, Mort again raised the question: Would she accept a tube? Unwavering, Milly said, "I'll do it." Mort was astonished at her change of heart. Milly had said she wanted to live! The tube improved her health and strength, Mort wrote in a follow-up edition of *Saving Milly*, but it had little effect on her speech, which was almost unintelligible. Around Christmastime of that year, Mort asked Milly about God, whom she felt had forsaken her, and she answered softly, "I love God. I talk to Him every day . . . He is the only one I can talk to whenever I want."

Prayer as a Simple Observation and Good Medicine

One Sunday morning 15 or so years ago when I was in Florida visiting my dad and my stepmother, many of my 11 step-siblings and their families also were there. Considering the logistics of getting everyone to church on that particular morning, including maybe 20 or 25 grandchildren in tow, Dad and Betty decided to have their own service out of doors on their patio. Betty suggested we sit in a circle and go around the group, identifying the things for which we were grateful. The responses, including mine, were more or less predictable: the family; the beautiful setting; our good health (at the time); and adequate food, clothing, and shelter for everyone.

Finally, it was Dad's turn. There was a long, thoughtful pause; then he cleared his throat and spoke.

"I'm grateful," he said, "for what is, perhaps, the greatest gift of all—the ability to appreciate."

I suggest that by way of appreciating and maybe *only* by appreciating (not through our heads but through our hearts) can we approach knowing something about that which is divine.

❀

Does prayer not only comfort patients but also aid them medically? Some researchers are saying yes.

In a 2003 *Washington Post Parade* article entitled "Why Prayer Could Be Good Medicine," several well-known academics look at spirituality and health. Professor Diane Becker of Johns Hopkins and a recipient of two NIH grants for research on prayer stresses, "We are not out to prove that a deity exists. We are trying to see whether prayer has meaning to people that translates into biology and affects a disease process."

Cited in the article are a new mushrooming of scientific investigations into faith and healing—a frontier for medical research.

At Duke University, a study of 4,000 men and women of various faiths found that the relative risk of dying was 46 percent lower for those who frequently attended religious services. In another study of the same group, researchers found that those who prayed regularly had significantly lower blood pressure than the less religious. A third study showed that those who attended religious services had healthier immune systems than those who did not. Dr. Harold Koenig, director of Duke's Center for Religion/Spirituality and Health, said of prayer, "It boosts morale, lowers agitation, loneliness and life dissatisfaction and enhances the ability to cope in men, women, the elderly, the young, the healthy and the sick." And says Duke's Dr. Mitchell Krucoff, "Nobody knows what really happens in human beings when they pray or when you pray for them in terms of the physiological mechanisms involved." Some scientists speculate that prayers may foster a state of peace and calm that could lead to beneficial changes in the cardiovascular and immune systems.

As for prayers said for the benefit of another person (distance, or intercessory, praying)—does it work? Findings are mixed. In a review of 23 studies of intercessory prayer involving 2,774 patients, published in the Annals of Internal Medicine, a positive effect was found in 57 percent of cases. The review concluded that the evidence merits further study.

Dr. Dale Matthews of Georgetown University, author of *The Faith Factor*, estimates that about 75 percent of studies of spirituality have confirmed health benefits.

※

So the question that arises is: Does God work on the sick ward? My short answer is: I don't know. I don't know if there is an Almighty, and if there is, what he (or she) (or it) is up to, and I don't think it's particularly important to know. We're not dealing with a cerebral matter here. What's most important, in my opinion, aren't beliefs but that in-the-heart, overwhelmingly indescribable feeling that resides there, waiting for your discovery . . . that peace that surpasses all understanding.

Around matters of believing versus knowing, I often get the heebie-jeebies. My uncomfortableness has to do with people who regard God as the Almighty, the Creator, the all-powerful, all-present, all-knowing . . . *and they think they know how God thinks.* To me, thinking that you can fit God Consciousness inside a human brain is like assuming you can cram an elephant into a Volkswagen. It doesn't work.

To help myself come to a clearer understanding of the matter of faith, I've divided the matter of knowing into five levels:

Level 1: **Knowing** . . . where unquestioned certainty shuts out conflicting facts and opinions . . . where people fight to hold on to their point of view, which, if taken to the extreme, sows the seeds of hatred.

Level 2: **Believing** . . . which acknowledges a shade of doubt.

Level 3: **Knowing you're believing** . . . which implies a level of self-awareness while still leaving the door open for belief.

Level 4: **Knowing you don't believe.**

Level 5: **Knowing you don't know.**

In a world at war with itself—so often over matters of ideology and theology—I submit that we humbly stick to Level 5 of what I call the Framework of Knowing and Believing—knowing that there's a limitless number of things we don't know.

What is a belief, that concept playing a central role in Levels 2, 3, and 4 of the Framework? A belief, simply put, is the acceptance of something as true. It isn't truth. It's the placing of our trust or confidence in something. At the extreme, every belief that we hold defends every other belief that we hold, making our entire thinking process rigid, filled to the point of overload and ripe for refutation. That being the case, nothing can lead to the loss of our spiritual equilibrium faster than a belief upended, by having operated from the perspective that something that isn't truth is truth. As long as we think a belief (ours!) is true and another belief (theirs!) is false, we'll be stuck in belief and not reality, and that, as I see it, is the source of many of our world's problems.

When we acknowledge a belief as a belief, we gain some power. We know we don't know, and we can, then—using our tiny human intelligences—revel in the joy of wonderment and awe. We can build confidently on the paltry bit of knowledge that we do know that we know.

Back to Aunt Harriet

So, did God have it in for Aunt Harriet? Was her illness God's will? How did she reconcile her divinely directed bitterness? Again, I don't know, but I like the thinking of writer Anne Lamott, who provides a clue. In her lovely book, *Traveling Mercies: Some Thoughts on Faith*, Lamott talks about a basic religious principle: God isn't here to take away our pain but to fill it with His (or Her) presence. While we may not often see evidence of it, says Lamott, the people of the world are surrounded by grace, which she describes as the force that infuses our lives and keeps letting us off the hook. "It is unearned love," she says, "the love that goes before, that greets us on the way . . .

"Grace is the light or electricity or juice or breeze that takes you from that isolated place and puts you with others who are as startled and embarrassed and eventually grateful as you are to be there . . .

"I do not at all understand the mystery of grace," says Lamott, "—only that it meets us where we are but does not leave us where it found us."

Perhaps Aunt Harriet came to know something about grace.

(By the way—somehow—prior to her death in her late 80s, Aunt Harriet and God did happily reach a peaceful accord.)

A Time for Laughing!

Ours is a particularly close-knit part of Vermont. We call our region Central Vermont, and it's the location of one of the state's bigger cities, our state capital, Montpelier. Yet with a population of about 8,000 people, it's the smallest capital city in the United States.

When the news out of the Middle East hit our community several years ago, many people around here were horror-struck.

Thirteen-year-old Yaakov (nicknamed Koby) Mandell, nephew and cousin of a well-known East Montpelier family, had been stoned to death along with his friend Yosef. The boys, Israelis, had skipped school on that awful day in May of 2001 to explore a cave near their Jewish settlement in occupied lands claimed by Palestinians. Searchers found their horribly bludgeoned bodies the next day.

Two years after the murders, Koby's mother, Sherri Mandell, wrote a book as a way to memorialize the boys and to deal with her profound grief. In her book *The Blessing of a Broken Heart*, Sherri talks—of all things—about the power of humor and, in particular, about the boys' senses of humor. To make her point, she recounts a story from the Babylonian Talmud about Elijah and the World-to-Come:

> *One day Elijah was in the marketplace. Rabbi Beroka strode up to him and said: "Show me somebody with olam ha ba, somebody who will attain the World-to-Come." Rabbi Beroka meant, show me somebody who has earned the right to live forever because he or she is on such a high level of godliness; show me somebody who will bask in God's radiance, who will be God's beloved. There were many Talmud scholars in the market, impeccably dressed in long robes and turbans. Rabbi Beroka thought that surely these men with their great learning would merit God's light and eternal life. Elijah shook his head no and said, "I'm sorry. There's nobody here like that." Rabbi Beroka stroked his beard in surprise. Then a pair of young men entered the market, talking and laughing, dressed in*

worn out, simple clothes. Elijah pointed to them and said: "Those men merit to live forever."

Rabbi Beroka went up to them and asked, "You merit to live forever. Why? Why you?"

The young men knew why. They responded: "We tell jokes and make sad people happy. We bring people together in peace and laughter."

To spark laughter, to elicit glee, can be an act of peace and great love.

Koby and Yosef died on a Tuesday and were buried on Wednesday, leaving only two days for mourning before *Shabbat* . . . the Sabbath. According to ancient oral tradition, Sherri explains, it is forbidden to mourn and be sad on *Shabbat*. Not knowing whether she could muster the strength to go to the weekly gathering and rise above her grief, she had a conversation with her friend Ruthie Gillis, whose husband, Shmuel, a hematologist who had worked with cancer patients, many of them Arab, had been murdered in a drive-by shooting. Ruthie told Sherri that Shmuel's funeral had been on a Friday, and she and the other mourners had had to return directly from the cemetery and enter *Shabbat*.

"The *Shabbat* after Shmuel was killed," Ruthie said, "was the highest *Shabbat* of our lives—people I loved were around me and there was singing and beauty and there was life. There was strength. There was love." Sherri followed Ruthie's urging to enter Shabbat and before long was laughing with everyone else at some kind of silliness about Wonder bread, about how Koby had tied up a babysitter who escaped by tickling him, and about Ruthie's new job fanning diners with palm fronds at a Roman-like restaurant. There was singing . . . lots of singing.

Sherri wrote about "the freedom of joy in our jokes, in our laughter, laughter that takes us up to another world."

The Anatomy of Laughter

Author and editor Norman Cousins made laughter a key part of his recovery from a life-threatening disease. In his highly regarded classic, *Anatomy of an Illness*, Cousins describes his experimentation with the therapeutic use of humor.

The long-serving *Saturday Review* editor explains in his book how he mobilized his body's natural healing capability using prolonged periods of laughter—among other therapies—to beat the odds of recovering from the crippling disease ankylosing spondylitis. One specialist said those odds could be as bad as 500:1.

Cousins believed that his resistance to toxins had been compromised by an overstressed endocrine system and that his general body chemistry had been altered for the worse by stress and other negative emotions. "The inevitable question arose in my mind," he said. "What about the positive emotions?"

Cousins began his treatments when *Candid Camera* TV show producer Allen Funt set up Cousins with a movie projector and films of his best gags. The Marx Brothers were next.

Cousins made the "joyous discovery" that 10 minutes of genuine belly laughter would give him blessed pain-free sleep for at least two hours. When he woke up, the projector went back on, and in many cases Cousins was able to get back to sleep. To determine whether laughter actually was affecting his body chemistry, his body's ability to fight inflammation was tested by taking sedimentation rate readings. There were small decreases in the rate at each check, and the decreases were cumulative.

"I was greatly elated," said Cousins, "by the discovery that there is a physiologic basis for the ancient theory that laughter is good medicine."

Taking Humor Seriously

A few months before his death in March of 2008 at the age of 94, my dad was bent over, reaching for a bottle of bourbon on a lower shelf of his family room bar. My stepmother, Betty, saw him begin to slide along the edge of the counter and, with her 85-pound body, unsuccessfully tried to block his fall. They both went down, and Dad's weight was enough to crush Betty's femur. With her screams ricocheting off the stucco walls, Dad, who was dazed and disoriented, couldn't walk but managed to scoot himself on his back across the big room to a phone and call for help.

Betty was rushed to the hospital and, following her surgery, had to endure a long, lonely stay until her rehabilitation was finished.

Throughout her recovery, Dad was merciless with himself. Everyone, it seems, tried to reason with him. There was no justification for him to fault himself, to blame himself, to smother in guilt. At the time of the accident, he actually hadn't had a drop to drink, he obviously loved Betty, and of course, he wouldn't have done anything to hurt her. But Dad wouldn't hear it.

Then, one day toward the end of his life, totally out of the blue, in his barely audible, worn-out voice, he whispered to me, "I didn't break the bottle."

He had healed.

✻

In the most challenging of situations, humor has shown its merit by providing the magic essential for creating a breakthrough and, ultimately, for transforming lives. Not infrequently, it is humor (and humor alone) that can detoxify poisonous, cynical, and resigned points of view. It is humor that can humanize us. It is humor that can enable us to see most anything in a new way.

Much humor requires the jettisoning of the heavy burden of significance heaped unnecessarily onto life.

Renowned Maine artist Robert Barnes told me a few years ago that he's received criticism from the fine arts community for his often uproarious paintings. The one that particularly caught my eye the day I met him was funny, mocking, attention-getting, and full of complex messages. At first glance, it was a simple picture of a dignified guy taking a pratfall, but there was more . . . themes ranging from class sensibilities to the nature (or absence) of empathy. "Humor," he says, "surreptitiously hooks you and pulls you in to deeper levels."

✻

Not long ago I saw a video of a stand-up comedy show featuring people who had something besides comedic talent in common. Each had a horribly disfigured face.

The troupe was outrageous, making on-the-edge jokes about their appearance. In time, faces that were hard, if not nearly impossible, for the audience to look at became something different: highly charged material for comedy routines that took everyone in the theater to a new level of acceptance, appreciation, respect . . . and love. At the end of the show, the audience was thunderous in its admiration and gratitude to a troupe of comics who had made peace with their own nightmares and come out of the process different from when they began it.

Many of the funniest people I've known have had little or no idea about the source of their humor. In fact, I think they've known on some level that if they understood the mechanics of humor, their humor would die. Part of the brilliance of humor is that it sneaks up on you from Who Knows Where and gets you. Humor is one of the Great Gifts. Funniness gets dropped into people's heads unbeknownst to them. It can shift a person's whole way of being without the person ever knowing it.

Humor also is risky business. To tell a joke or to make a witty quip requires gutsiness. The process calls for no holding back. It calls for generosity and trust on the part of the joker and openness on the part of the recipient. For humor to work, it takes attentiveness and vulnerability on the part of the listener as well as a certain affection for the listener . . . the desire of the joker to bestow a gift. Laughter can move a patient toward the threshold of transformation. After we've had a great laugh . . . one that makes us cough and choke, cry and gasp for breath . . . there's nothing left to do but savor the divinity of the experience.

Afterword

Last year, after many, many years of almost daily effort, my husband finished this book, a slim volume of life philosophy. Perhaps Bruce was prescient. Only weeks later, he was permanently stripped of his ability to write when he collapsed from a cerebral hemorrhage, which was eventually diagnosed as terminal brain cancer. He would never be able to write or read again, or think and express himself clearly. Bruce refers in his book to his Parkinson's disease as a footnote to his life. Brain cancer was not a footnote but a full stop.

A week after his collapse, Bruce underwent surgery to attempt to remove as much of the brain tumor as possible. It was a week before I thought he was healed enough physically and clear enough mentally to hear the news. I struggled to make it as simple and honest as possible.

"Honey, the doctors tell me that your brain tumor is very bad. You will not be in any pain and you do have some time, but the tumor is going to kill you." I held my breath while we stared at each other. He replied, "It's OK; I've had a wonderful life."

In retrospect I shouldn't have been surprised by his reaction, but because it was so stunningly different from the deep grief that had pierced me for days, I believed his response was delusional. Then it finally sunk in. He understood, and he meant what he said.

Bruce was a sick man almost from the beginning of our marriage. He writes about fearing I'd want to ditch him because of his Parkinson's disease diagnosis a year after we married. But he read me wrong, because I already knew in my soul that Bruce was a gift and a grace to my life. He exemplified how to grab the present moment, live for joy, and bring happiness and comfort to other people. Living with Bruce and Parkinson's disease was a preface to living with him dying of brain cancer. He never flinched, even in the face of death. And he remained unafraid of death. He talked readily with his family and friends about dying and how lucky he was to have had such a wonderful life. Bruce remained determined to grab all the joy that he could while he was alive. I asked him one day if he was in a state of grace—he answered yes.

Together we rode the rogue wave of cancer and its treatment: surgery, hospital stay, rehabilitation, chemotherapy, radiation. Bruce's mental clarity and his ability to move his body around varied day to day and were impossible to predict. He went from a wheelchair to a walker to a cane to walking on his own, and then back again. Eventually he needed a second brain surgery for the placement of a shunt to remove the pressure the tumor was putting on his brain. I learned to take solace in small victories. A day after the shunt surgery, Bruce climbed out of bed, took two steps on his own for the first time in months, looked at me in amazement, and we fell into each other's arms, crying.

Bruce writes in this volume, "We can cultivate genuine hope even when we are acutely aware that things are not going well and the likelihood of a good outcome is small. Hope is an ongoing choice." I had found that living with Bruce with Parkinson's disease was reason for hope for all of our 17 years together. But in face of the certain and rapidly approaching end to his life, I resented the sophomoric idea of hope. My resentments were specific and strange. Parkinson's disease and prostate cancer apparently was not enough for my good husband, he now had to endure a fatal brain tumor. I specifically resented the brain tumor because it was extinguishing his definition of himself—his ability to delight, entertain, and edify with words. It was erasing the word magician, the wit, the irascible, irrepressible optimist who could take any circumstance, including a dire one, turn it on its head, make a joke, and shift your perception.

A phrase from a Robert Frost poem brought me back to the place that Bruce dwelt in, "Hope does not lie in a way out, but in a way through." He was constantly giving others this kind of hope—a way to live fully, a way through suffering. He had become a symbol of hope for so many, especially in the Parkinson's community. And I realized finally that even words were not essential to Bruce's ability to delight and connect with others.

Up until the very end of his life, Bruce wanted to be with others. His community, our community, exemplified the African proverb, "The ladder of death is not climbed by only one person." We wanted for nothing from those who surrounded us daily—food, companionship, laughter, and music flowed to our family in our hour of need.

But it was a two way street. Bruce kept giving. Visitors climbed the stairs to his bedroom quiet, apprehensive, often scared, appropriate behavior and emotions that fit the scene of a dying man. They left him, however, shaking their heads and smiling. They had come to be with and comfort Bruce but found his sparkling spirit brought them just as much solace.

As I went through Bruce's dying, my overwhelming grief lived life in a parallel universe. I understood that everyday life continued around me, but I was estranged from it. I was repulsed by the smallness, the pettiness of much of normal life. News of the world was irrelevant to me. I couldn't tolerate for long any distraction from my grief.

I was aware of using all of my capacities all of the time—physical, emotional, and spiritual. I was bearing the unbearable, and it had more than a touch of the surreal. I was content with my own company, or only wanted to be in the company of people who understood, because of their own personal losses, or with a handful of friends I had been close with for decades. I simply put one foot in front of the other, hour after hour, day after day, week after week, month after month. Ordinary time warped. It contracted, expanded, sped up, and slowed down. Not knowing when Bruce would die, just knowing it was closer every day, was the most wrenching aspect, the most difficult to bear.

As Bruce's condition worsened, I became the center of the wheel for his 24/7 care. I knew that what was most important for him, and for me in his last months, was to be together. Just be. Talking, not talking, touching, not touching, it didn't matter. We held each other for hours, knowing the gift it was. On one of these occasions, Bruce and I looked at each other. "I'm happy," he said. "Me too," I replied. And we were.

Our partnership was strong and our joy in being together never diminished. At one point Bruce told me, "I married you forever, Judith. My dying doesn't change that." Of course, in his next breath, he joked, "So who's going to be your third husband?"

Bruce received home palliative and hospice care until what were the last three weeks of his life. On the last day of 2010 he was transferred by ambulance to a small, private hospice room, and I reluctantly handed over his daily care to the wise and competent staff. My task became very simple and almost impossible. I had to make peace with the inevitable, and simply be present, while I watched him die.

By now Bruce could barely speak. He didn't need comfort, but I had the need to comfort him. He had over the years told me that his meditation experience allowed him to see the beauty inside of himself. I told him, "Remember the beauty. Think of the beauty. That is where you are going."

In the final hours I leaned over him, "Sweetheart" escaping my lips, not expecting an answer. I was startled by the faint "Yes," I heard, Bruce responding without moving his mouth. He was so present for me, still. I climbed into bed with him for what was to be the final vigil. Our children surrounded us, and when he was ready, Bruce passed into the void in complete peace knowing his life mattered.

"I do not at all understand the mystery of grace," writes Annie Lamott in *Traveling Mercies: Some Thoughts on Faith*, "only that it meets us where we are but does not leave us where it found us." Bruce met me where I was, but he did not leave me where he found me. His most fervent hope for this book is that it will do the same for you.

– Judith Talbot Sutphen
June 2011

Acknowledgements

This book was a labor of love, not just for Bruce, but for many of his friends and loved ones.

Bruce left behind various lists of those who had taken the time to read, review, and often respond with extensive comments to the many versions of his book. Bruce took many of your suggestions to heart, and used them to continually hone the book's content.

In thanking some of you, I know I run the risk of unknowingly not including all. Please accept in advance my apologies for any omissions, as this list was finalized after Bruce had left us.

Much heartfelt thanks, among others, to the following readers: Marialisa Calta, Rickey Gard Diamond, David Eger, Alex Ellerson, Paul Erlbaum, Mary Flemming, Donna Fitch, Rhonda Freed, Rachael Grossman, Oliver Hall, Ray Holland, Sherry Lee, Jane Robb and Roger Strauss.

– Judith Talbot Sutphen
December 2011